Messy Vintage

15 The Chambers, Vineyard
Abingdon OX14 3FE
brf.org.uk

Bible Reading Fellowship is a charity (233280)
and company limited by guarantee (301324),
registered in England and Wales

ISBN 978 0 85746 975 5
First published 2021
Reprinted 2021
10 9 8 7 6 5 4 3 2 1
All rights reserved

Acknowledgements
Scripture quotations marked with the following abbreviations are taken from the
version shown. NKJV: The New King James Version®. Copyright © 1982 by Thomas
Nelson. Used by permission. All rights reserved. CEV: The Contemporary English
Version. New Testament © American Bible Society 1991, 1992, 1995. Old Testament
© American Bible Society 1995. Anglicisations © British & Foreign Bible Society
1996. Used by permission. NIV: The Holy Bible, New International Version (Anglicised
edition) copyright © 1979, 1984, 2011 by Biblica. Used by permission of Hodder
& Stoughton Publishers, a Hachette UK company. All rights reserved. 'NIV' is a
registered trademark of Biblica. UK trademark number 1448790. NRSV: The New
Revised Standard Version of the Bible, Anglicised edition, copyright © 1989, 1995 by
the Division of Christian Education of the National Council of the Churches of Christ
in the United States of America. Used by permission. All rights reserved. RSV: The
Revised Standard Version of the Bible, copyright © 1946, 1952, 1971 by the Division
of Christian Education of the National Council of the Churches of Christ in the United
States of America. Used by permission. All rights reserved. NLT: The Holy Bible, New
Living Translation, copyright © 1996, 2004, 2007, 2013. Used by permission of Tyndale
House Publishers, Inc., Carol Stream, Illinois 60188. All rights reserved. MSG: *The
Message*, copyright © 1993, 1994, 1995, 1996, 2000, 2001, 2002 by Eugene H. Peterson.
Used by permission of NavPress. All rights reserved. Represented by Tyndale House
Publishers, Inc.

Every effort has been made to trace and contact copyright owners for material used
in this resource. We apologise for any inadvertent omissions or errors, and would
ask those concerned to contact us so that full acknowledgement can be made in
the future.

A catalogue record for this book is available from the British Library

Printed and bound in Great Britain by TJ Books Limited, Padstow, Cornwall

Messy Vintage

52 sessions to share Christ-centred fun and fellowship with the older generation

Katie Norman and Jill Phipps

BRF

Contents

Foreword

Never did I imagine seven years ago that the form of 'doing church' which has become Messy Vintage would start to spread like wildfire and that I'd become such an advocate of it.

Messy Vintage started in Philadelphie Methodist Church in the parish of St Peter, Jersey, now a Messy Centre. That doesn't just mean they do Messy Church, they *are* a Messy Church. The then-minister, the Revd Christine Legge, and local lay minister Katie Norman explained how a few years ago the church was heading for closure. 'The congregation was dwindling. As they got older, it was harder and harder to find officers: people to be stewards and so on,' said Katie.

'We faced a stark choice,' explained Christine: 'Change or die.' Having held their first Messy Church in 2009, Katie had been praying that Messy Church might grow and become central to their plans. So, in 2011, building on the success of the Messy Church, Messy Vintage as we now know it went 'on the road' to local care homes. In the spring of 2013, a celebration service was held to 'praise God and give thanks for his vision for 'Philadelphie Messy Centre'.

They haven't looked back since. When I visited the church, across the hall-way, tables were laid for the fine tea which follows every Messy Vintage at the Centre. What a tea it was – gingham cloths, fresh roses in porcelain vases and an Indian tree-patterned tea service. Cake stands and doilies were ready to be brought out, laden with dainty sandwiches, cream and jam scones and all manner of fancy cakes.

In ones and twos the people arrived, some climbing off mobility scooters, men and women from sheltered homes and others who lived alone, some who had been given lifts to the centre and all gathering for friendship, fellowship and the promise of that delicious tea.

The atmosphere was more sedate than when children burst through the doors for Messy Church on other days of the week. The Messy team was ready in their aprons and with name badges to meet and greet every older person by name and guide the less mobile to their places. Gentle devotional music was playing in the background.

It opened with a welcome, some familiar hymns, then all settled down to a themed craft activity. This month the emphasis was on 'Pumping up – faith fitness'. We were each encouraged to make a mosaic reflecting something of our journey through life, of what is important to us, whatever we might be inspired to depict, using the different coloured tiles.

Later there was a talk on the Micah challenge (Micah 6:8). What does God require of you? 'To act justly, love mercy and walk humbly with your God.' The conversation over the choosing, gluing, sorting and snipping didn't flag.

Helpers guided those with less nimble fingers to complete their tasks, and all the while everyone was talking, swapping stories, evoking memories, laughing, giving and receiving gentle encouragement.

We were invited to show one another the results of our concentration. A man shows his tile – a mosaic with a cross in the middle, light radiating from it. Another man talks of a winding path, 'the ups and downs, twists and turns of life'. Another's has a cross too, this time with arms outstretched from it. 'It's about love,' the maker explains. A woman shows us her tile saying, 'The dark pieces are for the times of depression.' Everyone nods. I notice there are more light mosaic pieces than dark ones glued on her board.

It is not difficult to see the advantages of Messy Vintage. The activities are absorbing. The exchanges between us all were honest and authentic. People's self-esteem grows visibly through the loving attention they are paid. If friendship is top of the list of what churches should provide (when older people are asked for their opinion), Messy Vintage makes space for friendship aplenty.

In a care home I went to the next day for Messy Vintage 'on the road', few of the participants were able to colour in drawings for themselves depicting the Lord's Prayer. But that was no barrier to enjoyment, as people in wheelchairs selected the colours they wanted helpers to use, and discussed their memories of church as a child, or chatted about football, or how much they liked the music playing softly in the background.

One helper, on only her second time out as a team member, said, 'From the moment you come in here, it feels like you're entering sacred space. The atmosphere of peace is amazing.'

I helped one man in the lounge who had very little ability to speak. His intonation, the way he modulated his voice, might have sounded like that of normal, everyday, conversation. But only one word in about twenty was comprehensible. You might have thought it nigh on impossible for us to communicate. But gradually we did find a way to connect through smiles, having a hand to hold, a repetition of those words I did catch… to check with him that I'd understood correctly. When I bade him farewell, he took the name badge sticker off his shirt and gave it to me as a keepsake.

Since 2014 many other key people, like Katie, have been drawn into this endeavour. Jill Phipps lives not far from me in Hampshire and first contacted me because of her interest in Anna Chaplaincy for Older People. Again, little did she, or I, know we would come to be colleagues spreading the word of Messy Vintage which is now overseen by the Anna Chaplaincy team.

I was in Crickhowell in Powys, Wales, one day, talking about Messy Vintage, when a hand shot up and a man told me proudly how they conduct Messy Vintage in some care homes nearby. It seems you can't keep a good thing down. He was so keen to tell everyone assembled on that day all about it, at an event focusing on ministry among older people.

This book is the fruit of an irrepressible delight in the fact that God is doing something new. Such enthusiasm for it is infectious. Katie and Jill are a formidable duo, determination personified, when it comes to making church happen in some of the least likely places.

Let them guide you into the art of creating worship which touches all the senses and, quite simply, sets people free to be who God wants them to be.

Debbie Thrower
Anna Chaplaincy Pioneer

Find out more about Anna Chaplaincy at **annachaplaincy.org.uk**

Acknowledgements

Many people have had a part to play in bringing this book into existence. We are grateful to Richard, Debbie, Alex and Olivia at The Bible Reading Fellowship (BRF) for their initial suggestion to write it and for their, and Lucy's, ongoing encouragement while it was in progress. To Alex and Wendy, who read and made helpful suggestions on our first drafts, noticing the fine details which we had overlooked, and to Rachel and the BRF publishing team, who delivered it from PC to printed word with patience, kindness and professional expertise – thank you all.

The craft activities in this book have come from a variety of sources: some from previous sessions and others new; some suggested by family and friends, others sourced from the internet and sites which we have listed at the back under 'Resources'. For all of these we give thanks, but perhaps one of the greatest shout-outs has to go to our amazing teams, who make all things possible.

A huge thank you to Deacon Sally Wheadon and all the team at Philadelphie Messy Centre, Jersey, for your passion, creativity and total belief that Messy Vintage needs to reach every corner of the globe.

Particular thanks to Flis and Chris on the Portsmouth team, and to Juliet Helbren and Wendy Horn of St Barnabas Church, Swanmore, Hampshire, for their help, advice and Wendy's prayerful reflection for the Bible Sunday craft.

Also to the staff, activity coordinators and residents of the care homes, for their warm welcome, enjoyment and participation in worshipping our creator God with us.

Finally, massive thanks to our long-suffering and patient husbands, Bill and Martin, who dished out encouragement and cups of coffee and tea, with great dollops of belief that we could do it!

We hope you enjoy the book and pray that God will use it to bless your work with our wise and wonderful older generation.

Introduction

Katie Norman writes:

It started with cake stands – not even real ones, just the vision of them. Cake stands so beautifully dressed and adorned with home-made cakes and finger sandwiches that they displayed a feast fit for kings; and indeed the guests were royalty, for they were 'the silver-haired heads' on whom God places his 'crown of glory' (Proverbs 16:31, NKJV).

It was a beautiful picture and one that could easily have remained just that if it were not for the unwavering belief and support of my minister at the time, Revd Christine Legge, who gave Messy Vintage her blessing, rolled her sleeves up and, along with our amazing Messy team, developed and grew what has become a much treasured way of 'being church'. The steadfast faith of our small Sunday congregation also played a huge part. They selflessly gave up what had long been familiar to them and enabled Philadelphie Methodist Church to be developed as a Messy Centre, a place in which all generations of mixed abilities and needs can celebrate in comfort, with Christ-centred fun, fellowship and food – all led by people as passionate now as they were when we started.

The Messy Vintage gatherings with which I am involved grew out of an existing Messy Church, but this does not necessarily need to be the case. I have spoken with many people seeking to serve the 'silver-haired heads' who have no involvement with Messy Church but who, in common with the teams who lead that phenomenal model of church, have hearts filled with passion and zeal to shine the light of God into every corner. For us, this 'corner' takes the form of sharing Messy Vintage at the Messy Centre, in care homes and in dementia units. For you, it may well be that a community centre, a village hall or a retirement home is the setting best suited to the needs of those you feel called to meet with. The meeting place is not pivotal to Messy Vintage; what is crucial is the heart from which Messy Vintage flows and adherence to the Messy principles of creativity, hospitality and celebration.

Creativity, for the predominantly older generation for whom Messy Vintage is aimed, can seem daunting, with such a vast array of abilities to cater for. However, it has been our experience over the last ten years that it is not so much the craft itself that is important but the time spent creating it together and the conversations that ensue. Some of you may feel that the craft sessions offered in this book are too simple (or maybe too difficult), but they are not set in stone. Think of them as the middle C from which to play the right tune for your gathering, and then adjust them accordingly. They are ideas off which to bounce, not necessarily to create exactly as depicted. So too the ideas for team conversation and celebration: adjust them, delight in them and above all have fun.

As for hospitality, this again will differ according to where you are meeting. When we meet for Messy Vintage in our church setting, it will come as no surprise to you that we serve the aforementioned delicious feast on three-tier cake stands, all beautifully laid out on tables dressed with crisply laundered coverings and with flowers adorning the centre. Sadly, this is not usually possible to replicate when going into care homes and dementia units, so in such instances we run the session just before the residents have their lunch or afternoon tea.

Hospitality, of course, comes not only in the form of food, but in being welcoming and generous of spirit and love, and in these respects there are no Messy Vintage bounds! For Messy Vintage is a church that creates a sacred space where even those without a voice can engage and delight. It is where participation is encouraged, not perfection sought, and where the sound of laughter, singing and percussion instruments throngs the air. It is where I have witnessed a man with seemingly no communication skills thumb through an illustrated Bible with such reverence and beauty that his intimacy with God was tangible, and where I have seen people moved to dance in joyous abandon as their act of praise. It is a church where hearts, long broken, find solace, where friendships are formed and where, as one of our faithful participants puts it, 'you feel part of a big family'.

Many older people yearn to be part of a 'big church family' but, for reasons of age or mobility, cannot engage in the more formal way of being church. 'I don't always get to church now as the service is too long,' says a 91-year-old. 'The Messy Vintage service time is just the right length for me. Our afternoon tea is delicious.' When Messy Vintage goes out into the community, 'being family' is equally as important and evident. 'We love to encourage all staff, family and visitors to get involved. It creates a wonderful atmosphere,' remarks the ward sister, along with the activity coordinator of an adult mental health unit, who also acknowledges the value of supporting the residents' spiritual needs in a 'wonderful afternoon of love and friendship'.

Clearly, Messy Vintage means a great deal to all whom it embraces, be that in church or in a community setting, but none more so than to the activities coordinator of the care home who opened their door for our very first Messy Vintage, for she simply puts it like this: 'We love Messy Vintage. It's like a breath of fresh air!'

I pray that as you read this book you too will feel that 'breath of fresh air' equipping, enabling and encouraging you to start up, or continue to grow, your Messy Vintage.

How to run Messy Vintage

Jill Phipps writes:

First, **pray**! Prayer is the priority from the start and all the way through. If God has laid this on your heart, pray it into being. Having the support of your minister, Churches Together group or deanery in the area is wonderful; as well as prayer and volunteer support, there may be financial support available to help with purchasing the craft materials and the refreshments.

If you are starting a new Messy Vintage, we suggest that you gather a small team of volunteers who have a heart for older people and are good listeners. This core team will be able to pray and help with the overall organisation needed to bring your Messy Vintage sessions together. A further team of volunteers, who will bring with them a variety of gifts and talents, can then be drafted in – those with artistic, creative, musical or catering skills are perhaps the most obvious, but those who can give practical help to set up and clear away are invaluable and precious too. If you can include young people in your team and members of other churches or denominations – or those who belong to no denomination – that is excellent, as this will bring a rich tapestry of input. Usually a team of five to ten people is sufficient to run a session, but you will know best what suits your group. There is a volunteer role description in Appendix II, if that helps.

The tasks for the core team include setting dates and times, deciding on the venue, planning the sessions and buying the craft materials and refreshments. You will also need to think about how you are going to publicise your Messy Vintage. Putting up posters in the local area, giving information via the churches or interviews on local radio or in newspapers, and using social media can all be effective ways of reaching both older people and their families. Your team will need current and relevant DBS certificates and need to have completed safeguarding training, according to your organisation's or denomination's guidance.

Second, the **venue**. Messy Vintage works across a range of different settings and is very adaptable, although it should always be offered on a sustainable time scale – less can be more! We recommend that, like Messy Church, you aim for once a month.

If your chosen venue is a community hall, is it on a bus route? Is there adequate parking? Could you offer transport, and if so who will organise that? Is it easily accessible for older people? Are the toilets close to the main space and safe? Other things to check would be whether there is level flooring, good lighting, heating and ventilation and comfortable chairs (ensure some have arms), along with space to move around and good kitchen facilities. Does the venue have public liability insurance and a fire safety policy? Have you carried out an appropriate risk assessment for the event? These are all things to be considered.

If you're holding Messy Vintage in a sheltered housing venue, the first person to speak to is the manager or warden. When meeting together, it is useful to take with you some written information on what Messy Vintage is, the length of the sessions, proposed dates, what is involved, team contact details and what would be required from the manager/warden. Following discussion and agreement on convenient dates and times and the appropriate space (e.g. the lounge), a poster or flyers advertising the first session are useful to leave with the manager to publicise the event and gain an idea of interest from the residents.

Similarly, the manager is the first person to contact when approaching a care home. It is useful to check beforehand if other churches or denominations already go in. Always explain that Messy Vintage is 'creative worship' for older people, not simply a craft activity, and emphasise that family members and staff are most welcome to join in too. Care homes welcome opportunities for spiritual nourishment for their residents and will support this different way of 'being church'. Activity coordinators are also key people in helping Messy Vintage to thrive in a care home setting, and they may be able to help in providing some resources for the craft, e.g. glue sticks, paper or instruments for the worship. We have developed a 'Memorandum of Understanding' (see Appendix I), which can help to clarify what is being offered and also what is required. The memorandum is there for you to amend the details for your own situation. The team should familiarise themselves with the home's routines, e.g. signing in and out, and its fire procedures, and always refer to the care staff if in doubt.

Third, the **craft**: this is an important part of the session and is a key time for conversation to flow, so a good number of volunteers are needed to provide support. George Bernard Shaw is quoted as saying, 'We don't stop playing because we grow old, we grow old because we stop playing.' The craft session is a time to have fun – childlike not childish – to unlock memories, to enjoy creating something, to 'have a go' or simply sit and enjoy watching others while being part of the conversation. The crafts are not intended to be works of art, but springboards for thought and reflection, reminders in the days ahead of that link to God that was the Messy Vintage theme. Good-quality resources are essential – this is not 'junk modelling'.

The crafts in this book have been inspired by and developed from various sources – our own thoughts and things we have tried before, conversations with friends, ideas on the internet and on Pinterest, with the aim of providing activities to cater for a wide range of different levels of dexterity and cognitive ability. You may wish to have a couple of different activities to cater for all, or just have one. In a care home setting, you may wish to make a joint craft, e.g. the Advent wreath or the Epiphany mobile, which could be displayed in a reception area or lounge for all to see and enjoy. It is also helpful in a care home or sheltered housing setting to have a poster explaining the theme and the craft of that session, as a further reminder and explanation of what goes on at Messy Vintage.

The celebration service typically lasts 15–20 minutes and you should aim to include a scripture reading (which we recommend that you read holding a Bible, as many older people find this to be a very reverent and familiar format), hymns and/or music and prayers. You may also wish to light a candle (LED if in a care home), have a small cross on the table or have holding crosses, a small vase of flowers or a model of praying hands – all these can help to transform the table into an altar and the room into sacred space. If your team includes musicians, you will be able to have live music; if not, a CD player, an MP3 player or a mobile phone with a Bluetooth speaker, or similar, work well.

In community settings, providing a printed order of service, including the words of the reading and the hymns, enables all to follow without hymn books, and it can then be taken home as a reminder of the session. In care homes, it is essential to choose well-known hymns and choruses, as many people will know them by heart, and this prevents confusion with lots of bits of paper or not having the right glasses! Ask for requests for prayer and remember to include them, and allow space for guests to pray aloud if they wish to. Always include the Lord's Prayer and the Grace (the Messy Church version, using appropriate actions, can be used if deemed suitable). This will bring the service to a peaceful end.

Refreshments are also a vital part of a Messy Vintage session. In care home settings, we often cannot provide the refreshments, but do try to fit in with their usual routine and timings. It may be that coffee or tea and cake come around during the craft activity or that residents go for their lunch as Messy Vintage finishes – if that is the case, could you offer to say grace before they start their meal? In community settings, the refreshments should be offered in the way that Katie describes in her vision for Messy Vintage at the start of this introduction – pretty tablecloths and serviettes, small vases of flowers, china crockery and lots of beautifully presented sandwiches and cakes all make it special. If you don't have space to set up the tea tables separately ahead of time, ensure there are enough volunteers to clear the craft tables quickly and to distribute the tea. If you have willing bakers, try to over-cater so that you don't run out of food, and you will be able to send people home with a 'goodie bag'. Remember to offer vegetarian and gluten-free choices, as well as different hot and cold drinks.

On the day, unless requested not to do so, ensure you have name badges for all and that team members are identifiable with a different colour badge or apron. In care homes, arrive in good time to set up and be ready to welcome residents as they arrive. In community settings, ensure you have sufficient volunteers to prepare the room and to set out the tables and chairs, and check that there is clear signage to the toilets. A warm welcome at the door, assistance with registration and familiar music playing in the background help to set the scene and provide an inviting atmosphere.

In community settings, you should decide what information you are going to collect from your guests. This may include: address and telephone numbers, birthdays, next of kin, emergency contact numbers, particular difficulties (e.g. sight, hearing or mobility), medications they may need to keep with them (e.g. inhalers) and permission (or not) for photographs. You will need to check your organisation's or denomination's data protection guidance, but this information will help to ensure that everyone can enjoy the session and that extra help can be provided for a guest where needed. Consider what information you would like guests to take away – dates and themes of forth-coming sessions and contact details of the team leaders as a minimum, but perhaps also information about other events they may be interested in and able to get to. Think about how you will collect feedback. Are you able to keep in contact with your guests between Messy Vintage sessions to develop that sense of belonging to a family? Ensure you ring anyone who misses a session or is not able to come to the next one. Remember and celebrate birthdays and keep in touch.

There are times in the year when opportunity arises for intergenerational Messy Vintage, particularly Christmas and Easter, but also in the summer. Many of our sessions and crafts can be adapted to include children and older adults, and this would be wonderful. However, they do need careful planning, preparation and additional volunteers to ensure that children and adults are safe and happy.

Finally, when the session has finished, the guests have gone home or off to their meal and the tables and chairs have been cleared away, have a team debrief or fix in your diaries a time soon after to do so. Discuss how the session went. What went well? What improvements could be made? Conclude with prayer, and continue to hold your guests and each other in prayer during the following weeks.

We hope you will enjoy this book and find it useful. We finish with the Anna Chaplaincy prayer:

Faithful God, you have promised in Christ to be with us to the end of time. Come close to those who have lived long and experienced much. Help them to continue to be faithful, and within the all-age kingdom of God, to find ways to go on giving and receiving your grace, day by day. For your glory and your kingdom. Amen

You can find downloadable templates and photos of the activities at **messychurch.org.uk/messy-vintage**. Downloadable templates are indicated by the PDF symbol.

OLD TESTAMENT

1
Mega God, micro me

Bible passage

Genesis 1:26–31

Focus verse

God created humans to be like himself.
GENESIS 1:27 (CEV)

Aim

To consider the enormity of what it means to live in God's image and the small things we can do that make a difference.

Messy team conversations

Talk about initiatives aimed at tackling environmental issues, such as recycling or community projects. Talk about travel: places people have visited, places on their bucket lists or cultural differences people have come across. Talk about food miles, countries where there are food shortages, food banks and soup kitchens.

Activity

 You will need: a copy of the 'Mega God, micro me' template for each person, printed on medium or heavy card; light and dark blue tissue paper; various seeds and lentils in small containers; PVA glue and glue spreaders; coloured pencils

Tear the tissue paper into small pieces and paste them on to the sea areas of the worksheet. Glue seeds and lentils on to the areas that represent the land mass. Draw your 'self' in the small box using coloured pencils.

Celebration

Read Genesis 1:26–31. Consider what it means to be created 'in God's image'. Do we reflect his love in our everyday lives?

If facilities allow, show a clip about Fairtrade (available from **youtube.com/ user/Fairtradefoundation**). Alternatively, you may wish to invite someone from an organisation in your area to talk about a project in which they are involved. Encourage interactive sharing about community projects: recycling centres, food banks, soup kitchens, shelters for the homeless, etc.

Display a large world map or a globe. Give each person a Post-it note and invite them to write or draw a picture of their prayer for either a particular area/person or for a worldwide situation, then stick the notes on the map/ globe and pray.

Prayer

Mega God, you made us to live in your image and gave us your blessing to care for your world, help us to recognise that, no matter how small we may feel, we can make a difference. Amen

Song suggestions

- How great thou art
- He's got the whole world in his hands
- Think of a world without any flowers
- Lord, the light of your love is shining (Shine, Jesus, shine)
- Lord, for the years your love has kept and guided

2

Creation celebration

Bible passage

Genesis 1:1–3, 20

Focus verses

In the beginning, God created the heavens and the earth… God saw all that he had made, and it was very good.

GENESIS 1:1, 31 (NIV)

Aim

To praise God for his creation, and its beauty, diversity and complexity.

Messy team conversations

Do you have a favourite place outdoors? Do you prefer the countryside or the beach? Enjoy sharing memories of holidays or walks. What is your favourite bird and why? Birds are mentioned a lot in the Bible. How many can you think of? What can we do to help look after God's world?

Activity

You will need (pipe-cleaner bird feeder): 30 cm pipe cleaners (any colour); a packet of Cheerios breakfast cereal; ribbon/ coloured string
You will need (apple bird feeder): apples; sticks approx. 25 cm long (two for each apple); sunflower seeds; apple corer

For the pipe-cleaner bird feeder, thread Cheerios loops on to the pipe cleaner, leaving 2.5 cm at each end free. Twist the ends together securely, ensuring they are well tucked under and won't hurt the birds. Loop a ribbon or string through to hang them in the trees.

For the apple bird feeder, core each apple. Thread a piece of string through the centre of the apple and tie it to a stick placed horizontally under the apple. Push another stick through the centre of the apple itself. Stick sunflower seeds into the apple skin. Hang up in the trees for the birds.

Celebration

Thanks to David Attenborough and many other TV presenters, we are more familiar with the beauty, complexity and diversity of God's creation.

Read Psalm 19:1–6 and give thanks and praise to God for his handiwork.

If possible, listen to a few minutes of a recording of 'The lark ascending' by Vaughan Williams and enjoy spending time with God.

Prayer

We praise you, Creator God, for all that you have made, for your loving care for all creation. Help us to care for and use the earth's resources wisely and well for the benefit of all of us who share it. Amen

Song suggestions

- All things bright and beautiful
- Morning has broken
- All creatures of our God and king
- How great thou art
- He's got the whole world in his hands

3

God's rainbow promise

Bible passage

Genesis 9:8–17

Focus verse

> God said, 'This is the sign of the covenant I have established between me and all life on the earth.'
> GENESIS 9:17 (NIV)

Aim

To bring hope and comfort to people.

Messy team conversations

Talk about your experiences of seeing rainbows. How do rainbows make you feel? Have fun trying to recall the words to the song 'I can sing a rainbow'.

Activity

 You will need: a copy of the rainbow template for each person, printed on blue card; seven small balls of wool in, as near as possible, the colours of the rainbow; glue sticks or PVA glue and spreaders; green crêpe paper, crinkled paper or similar; cotton wool balls; scissors

In advance: cut the wool into strands of around 25–40 cm, or cut all the strands to 40 cm so that people can choose their own sequence of colours.

On the day: stick sufficient strands of wool to cover each sector of the rainbow (on average four strands works best). Cut off any excess wool and secure a band of green crêpe paper to cover the raw edges and form the grass. Stick cotton wool clouds in the sky.

Note that this is a beautiful but quite fiddly craft, so make sure you have enough ready hands available, especially if you are on a tight schedule.

Celebration

Talk about the story of Noah and the flood, giving opportunity for people to participate in the telling of it. Read Genesis 9:8–17.

A covenant is a binding relationship rooted in commitment and faithfulness between all parties. God sent his covenant promise of hope through Noah as a symbol of peace and harmony.

Use the craft pictures to prompt people to share ways in which they feel God's promise gives them hope and comfort, and consider our spiritual response to God's promise and our covenant with him.

Prayer

Faithful and everlasting God, we thank you for the beauty of rainbows reminding us of your promise to us and all life on earth, bringing us not only joy and delight, but also comfort and hope for ourselves and for your hurting world. Amen

Song suggestions

- O, Jesus I have promised
- Praise to the Lord, the almighty
- With gladness we worship, rejoice as we sing
- New every morning is the love
- O give thanks to the Lord, all you his people

4

God's provision

Bible passage

Exodus 2:1–6, 9–10

Focus verse

'Take this baby and nurse him for me, and I will pay you.'
EXODUS 2:9 (NIV)

Aim

To reflect on God's provision for us.

Messy team conversations

One of the names of God in the Old Testament is Jehovah Jireh – God provides. How has God provided for you over the years?

Activity

You will need: sheets of coloured paper, minimum 22 cm square; card heart shapes 7 cm long and wide (available from Hobbycraft); pens; stickers and other items to decorate the basket with

Start by folding the square in half and opening it up again, side to side, up/down and diagonally. Fold two opposite corners to meet in the middle. Fold these again to the middle and stand them up – they become the sides of the basket. At each end, take the sides that slope down, push on them and flick the pointed end up. Fold it up and over so that the point meets the other points inside the bottom of the basket. Repeat at the other end. You should have a neat basket!

Take the heart shapes and write on them the things that God has provided for you throughout your life, then place them in the basket.

Ensure the team are familiar with how to make this craft beforehand. If you're stuck, there is an eight-step guide for an origami basket at **wikihow.com/ Make-an-Origami-Paper-Basket**.

Celebration

The story of Moses in the basket reminds us of our fragility and vulnerability in the world, yet God was watching over the baby and ensured he grew up safe and strong.

Share some examples of God's provision in our times of need and spend some time praising him.

Prayer

End your worship by saying the Lord's Prayer together.

Song suggestion

- Praise, my soul, the king of heaven
- Jehovah Jireh, my provider
- Lord, for the years
- Tell out my soul
- Seek ye first the kingdom of God

5

Blessings

Bible passage

Numbers 6:22–26

Focus verse

'The Lord bless you and keep you.'
NUMBERS 6:24 (NIV)

Aim

To remember how God has blessed us and to pass on that blessing to others around us.

Messy team conversations

Chat about blessings, gifts and good things in life. Have you heard about the film *Pay It Forward*, about a young boy who comes up with an idea to pass on favours?

Activity

You will need: lolly sticks about 15 cm long; glue; wool in different colours; scissors; small self-adhesive mirror tiles (optional); ribbon

Ojo de Dios (God's eye) is a yarn weaving of wool and wood, often with several colours. It is an ancient contemplative and spiritual practice for many indigenous peoples in the Americas. Ojo de Dios have traditionally been created for celebration or blessing, presented as a gift or designed to bless a home. Often they reflect confidence in all-seeing Providence.

There are good videos on the internet to show how to make Ojo de Dios, and we recommend that the team familiarise themselves with how to do it ahead of the session.

The lolly sticks should be glued into a cross shape beforehand. Start with one colour of wool and wind it around the sticks to form the central 'eye', following with at least two other colours. Secure the ends of the wool and make a loop with which to hang the 'God's eye'. If you wish, you can fix a mirror tile on the innermost colour.

Celebration

Read Psalm 103:1–2. Spend time praising God and thanking him for all his goodness to us.

Pray for those who need God's blessing.

Prayer

Heavenly Father, we praise you and thank you for your great goodness to us. Help us not to forget all you have done for us. We love you, Lord. Amen

If possible, end the worship session by listening quietly to 'The Lord bless you and keep you' by John Rutter.

Song suggestions

- Thank you, Lord, for this fine day
- Give thanks with a grateful heart
- Count your blessings
- 10,000 reasons (Bless the Lord)
- Praise, my soul, the king of heaven
- Great is thy faithfulness

6

Balaam's donkey

Bible passage

Numbers 22:21–38

Focus verse

'I must speak only what God puts in my mouth.'
NUMBERS 22:38 (NIV)

Aim

To highlight that our ways are not always God's way.

Messy team conversations

Has anyone led or ridden a donkey? What was it like? Who likes doing things their own way? Is it always right? What have some of the consequences of that been, both funny and more thought provoking?

Activity

 You will need: a copy of the donkey craft template for each person, printed on thin card; an A4 sheet of thin card per person, with a ruled frame for them to create their own border or with a downloaded printed border; felt-tip pens or coloured pencils; pencil sharpener; wool; googly eyes; scissors; glue sticks or PVA glue and spreaders

Colour in the donkey shapes and cut them out, assemble them on the A4 card and stick them into place. Attach the googly eyes and form a forelock of wool hair. Draw a border to form a frame.

Celebration

Share thoughts on the characteristics of donkeys, or better still arrange for someone to bring a donkey in! Donkeys have a reputation of being stubborn but are also very loyal, calm and gentle.

Tell the story of Balaam's donkey in your own words, based on Numbers 22:21–38.

To Balaam, the donkey appeared stubborn – to God, Balaam did! We too can be sometimes stubborn and do things that we know God would not choose for us to do. As a result we can hurt the very people who are trying to help us. We need to pray and seek God's heart before we act and speak.

Prayer

Almighty and powerful God, help us not to stubbornly go our own way but to seek your presence in our lives, guiding us and giving us the words that you want us to speak. Amen

Song suggestions

- Dear Lord and Father of mankind
- Make me a channel of your peace
- May the mind of Christ my Saviour
- When we walk with the Lord
- Be thou my vision

7

Facing our giants

Bible passage

1 Samuel 17:40–50

Focus verse

'The battle is the Lord's.'
1 SAMUEL 17:47 (NIV)

Aim

To encourage people to give their fears over to the Lord, in prayer.

Messy team conversations

Talk about things that some people find really difficult to conquer, e.g. going in lifts, travelling, talking in public or going to the dentist. Gently invite people to share any fears they may have, but be sensitive and don't force conversation. Leave space for silent thoughts while doing the craft.

Activity

You will need: large painting pebbles (7–8 cms); acrylic gloss paints or acrylic pens (metallic porcelain pens work well on stone); fine and medium paint brushes plus water pots if using paint; kitchen roll

Decorate the pebbles however you wish.

Celebration

Talk about fears and how they can seem like giants in our lives. Ask if anyone knows the story of David and Goliath. Use the input to tell the story or give the background of the story yourself to the point of the head-on battle, then read 1 Samuel 17:40–50.

Finish by emphasising how small we can feel in the face of the things that seem huge in our lives, our giants, but when we offer them to God in prayer, he will help us to overcome them.

Prayer

Invite people to look at their stone while you pray:

Victorious and almighty God, we bring to you our giants of fears and anxieties, trusting that, like David, as we hand the enormity of them over to you, you will overcome them – for the battle is yours, and you will be victorious. Amen

Song suggestions

- In heavenly love abiding
- Father, I place into your hands
- Fight the good fight with all thy might
- How sweet the name of Jesus sounds
- God sent his Son, they called him Jesus
- Jesus – the name high over all

8

Prayer walking

Bible passage

Psalm 1:1–3

Focus verse

Their delight is in the law of the Lord, and on his law they meditate day and night.
PSALM 1:2 (NRSV)

Aim

To help us in our walk with God.

Messy team conversations

Chat about different ways of praying – perhaps on a lovely walk through the woods, by the sea or around the neighbourhood praying for residents. Or at home, using the news or an app on a phone or tablet. How we pray will be affected by our personality – introverts often find it easier than extrovert characters to sit and be still.

Activity

 You will need: the labyrinth templates, printed on A4 paper; light card; crayons, watercolours; laminator (optional)

Labyrinths are ancient pathways. Each one is a single pathway (not a maze) which turns and curves in a pattern around a central point; the start and end points are the same. There are many in the world, in churchyards and cathedrals. Pilgrims have come to walk them for many years. Finger labyrinths can be used for prayerful reflection when it is not possible to walk a full-sized labyrinth.

Colour or paint the labyrinth paths, using different colours – it will be easier to follow the path with your finger. If you wish, you could then laminate it. A fabric labyrinth may be made by transferring a pattern on to a piece of plain material or Binca weave and using embroidery threads to stitch along the lines. The completed finger labyrinth could be made into a cushion or simply laid on top of a cushion for use.

'Walking' the labyrinth is a three-stage process, using a finger:

- Opening your heart and mind to God as you enter
- Time for reflection when reaching the centre
- Journeying outwards with insights gained.

Celebration

Share the different ideas about praying. There may be something you could try for a change. Spend time praising God for his goodness.

Prayer

God of all our journeys, you are the way, the truth and the life. Thank you that you walk alongside us in everything we do, say and see, and help us to share your love with everyone we meet. Amen

Song suggestions

- Lead us, heavenly Father, lead us
- When we walk with the Lord
- Abba Father
- Be still for the presence of the Lord
- The Spirit lives to set us free

9

Our God is a great, big God

Bible passage

Psalm 34:1–3

Focus verse

O magnify the Lord with me, and let us exalt his name together!
PSALM 34:3 (RSV)

Aim

For friends and family, or maybe a school class, to share in a time of fun and fellowship as you praise the Lord at a Messy Vintage bug drive! This session could be used as a follow-up to 'A surprise invitation' (session 28).

Messy team conversations

The conversations around the table will play out organically.

Activity

 You will need: sufficient quantities of yellow, green, red and grey playdough; standard black pipe cleaners; fine black pipe cleaners or other suitable material for use as legs and feelers; small scraps of tinsel pipe cleaners; coloured feathers; googly eyes; black felt-tip pens; dice and shaker pots, one for each table; a copy of the 'Instructions to play' template for each table; a few small prizes, such as bars of chocolate or soap; a person (the caller) to direct the game

Sit people at tables of no more than six. Explain that each player is playing for themselves (not in pairs). Hand out the instructions and give out the component parts needed for whichever bug you are using. To play, each player throws the dice, making up their insect when the correct number is thrown. They continue to throw the dice until a number is thrown for a piece they already have. The game then moves on to the player on their left until someone finishes and shouts 'bug'. After a small prize is given out, move on to the next bug. (Note: You could shorten the games by allowing multiple pieces per correct throw; e.g. throw six to get all the legs.)

Celebration

Read Psalm 34:1–3. Talk about the power of placing magnification on even the smallest of insects. Whether by using a magnifying glass or viewing it on a nature programme, the end result is the same: what is revealed is a beauty and intricacy beyond what we could possibly imagine.

In the same way, if we want to see the beauty and intricacy of God, we need to magnify him. Not by trying to make God bigger than he truly is, for that would be impossible, as God is greater than all things, but by making God bigger in us, in our whole being – in our thoughts, actions, hearts and praise. In these ways we magnify God and see his intricate beauty and utter awesomeness.

Prayer

We thank you, our great, big, awesome God, for this time of fun, fellowship and praise. May we magnify you in our daily lives and never cease to tell everyone of your intricate beauty. Amen

Song suggestions

- Our God is a great big God
- How great thou art
- Our God is an awesome God
- Immortal, invisible, God only wise
- Praise to the Lord, the almighty
- With gladness we worship, rejoice as we sing

10

A New Year song

Bible passage

Psalm 96:1–3

Focus verse

Sing to the Lord a new song.
PSALM 96:1 (NIV)

Aim

To share God's glory with fresh vibrancy and joy.

Messy team conversations

Talk about experiences of the past year and the hopes and dreams of things to come in the new year. Talk about New Year's resolutions made and broken!

Activity

You will need: an A4 year-view calendar blank card per person; an A5 sheet of white card; recycled wrapping paper, used cards or other suitable collage paper; glue sticks; scissors; fine felt-tip pens; highlighter pens; ribbon; sticky tape

In advance: write the letters 'M' and 'V' in bubble writing and make sufficient card stencils to share.

On the day: using the stencils, draw around the letters 'M' and 'V' on A5 card. Cut out desired shapes from the collage paper and stick them on to the letters. When completed, cut out the letters and stick them on to the A4 calendar. Colour in the border if it is already printed on the card or create a border. Highlight the dates that your Messy Vintage meets throughout the year. Cut a ribbon hanger and tape it into place.

Celebration

Read Psalm 96:1–3. How does this passage sit alongside our hopes and dreams for the new year? Have we resolved to sing a new song and declare God's glory with the same beauty and gusto as we hear in birdsong?

Listen to a recording of birdsong. There are numerous choices on YouTube and many audio CDs available. If you have the opportunity to go into or do this session in a garden, better still!

Think about how freely birds declare God's wonders. Invite the gathering to share ways in which we too can tell of God's love for us and his righteous rule throughout the earth 24/7.

Prayer

Glorious God, most worthy of our praise, help us to sing of your glory with fresh hearts and voices, that all may know of your greatness and love. Amen

Song suggestions

- Come, let us all unite to sing
- Let all the world in every corner sing
- To God be the glory, great things he hath done!
- New every morning is the love
- How great thou art
- Great is thy faithfulness

11

Shout for joy!

Bible passage

Psalm 100:1–5

Focus verse

> Shout with joy to the Lord, all the earth!
> PSALM 100:1 (NLT)

Aim

To worship with pure joy and adoration.

Messy team conversations

Where are sunflowers seen – in gardens and fields, printedon soft furnishings and tableware, and depicted in artwork? Discuss the uses of sunflower products – oil, seeds, body and hair products, seedcake for animal feed.

Activity

 You will need: copies of the sunflower heads, leaves and stalks templates; sheets of coloured A3 sugar paper; yellow, orange and green paint; paintbrushes; water pots; kitchen roll; scissors; black sunflower seeds or any flat seeds; PVA glue and spreaders; glue sticks; Bibles (optional)

Paint the petals of the flower heads, the leaves and the stalks. Once dry, cut them out and stick them on to a coloured sheet of A3 sugar paper. Mix a small amount of glue with some orange paint, then paint the centre of the flowers and sprinkle with sunflower seeds. Write 'Shout with joy to the Lord, all the earth!' on the finished picture – more verses or words from Psalm 100 could be added, in which case ensure you have Bibles available.

Celebration

If possible, take in some fresh sunflowers or hold up some of the artwork and think about how they make us feel. They really shout with joy and cause us to smile. Think about from where they get this joyous energy and what we can we learn from them.

A sunflower, no matter where it is rooted, turns itself in position so as to directly receive the sun's gaze. It shouts for joy, not at us, but at its creator. It symbolises adoration, loyalty and also longevity, for not only does the sunflower worship God but it provides for us and other creatures too.

Read Psalm 100:1–5. Have an interactive time sharing how the sunflower fulfils its God given purpose and how joyously it praises. How do we live out our praise and purpose? How can we spread the seeds of our faith?

Prayer

Creator God, with our faces turned to you we join with all the earth and shout for joy at the wonder of your unfailing love and faithfulness. Help us to be the fullness of your creation, spreading goodness and causing others to turn to you. Amen

Song suggestions

- As we seek your face
- Praise to the Lord, the almighty
- All people that on earth do dwell
- All things praise thee, Lord most high
- With gladness we worship, rejoice as we sing
- Now thank we all our God

12

This is me!

Bible passage

Psalm 139:1–4, 23–24

Focus verse

Search me, God, and know my heart; test me and know my anxious thoughts.
PSALM 139:23 (NIV)

Aim

To recognise that God is with us through all things and knows us from the inside out. It is through him and in him that we are made alive!

Messy team conversations

Take in some old photographs and downloaded images of Victorians and Edwardians. Talk about clothes, hairstyles, poses, etc. Take in some very modern pictures, maybe showing tattoos, piercings or face art, and share thoughts.

Activity

You will need: a sheet of heavy A3 paper for each person; mirrors (optional); pencils; rubbers; pencil sharpeners; paint; paintbrushes; small art palettes or old saucers; water pots or jam jars; kitchen roll or old rags

If appropriate to the gathering, work in pairs and have fun painting a portrait of each other or paint a self-portrait (you may wish to provide mirrors). You could use coloured chalks or another suitable medium.

Celebration

Delight in sharing the finished portraits and discuss how much we can learn about each other by just looking at an image. Think about the importance of friendships and relationship. Ask if anyone, no matter how precious to us, can truly know our heart apart from God.

Read Psalm 139:1–4, 23–24 or, if the gathering is suited to it, read the psalm in its entirety.

Prayer

All-knowing and all-seeing God, you are the only one who knows us perfectly, far beyond the knowledge of ourselves, our actions, our undertakings, our words and even our thoughts. Search our hearts, we pray, O Lord, and deliver us from all anxiety, that we may truly be the masterpiece that you have created us to be. Amen

Song suggestions

- O love that wilt not let me go
- Lord of all hopefulness
- I need thee every hour
- All to Jesus I surrender
- Guide me, O thou great Jehovah
- Give me joy in my heart

13

Wise sayings

Bible passage

Colossians 3:16

You could also choose a selection from Proverbs.

Focus verse

'As for God, his way is perfect: the Lord's word is flawless.'
2 SAMUEL 22:31 (NIV)

Aim

To encourage each other to share God's word with the same enthusiasm and delight as the way in which we share secular sayings gathered over the years, and to recognise that many of our familiar sayings come from a biblical route.

Messy team conversations

This session offers the opportunity to share much delight as old sayings are recalled. Talk about memories of how these sayings were lived out and the people from whom they were learnt.

Activity

 You will need: the owl body, wings and eye templates; coloured funky foam; pre-prepared labels (from the template) 'Wise sayings'; scraps of funky foam to make triangular feathers and a beak; googly eyes; split pins;

**thin ribbon; PVA glue and glue spreaders or glue sticks; sticky
tape; scissors; five or six large natural lolly sticks per person,
taped together with masking tape concertina fashion to allow
folding; pens**

In advance: print the template of the owl shapes and pre-cut all the parts
out of the funky foam. Or, if your group is able, provide enough stencils for
everyone to cut their own. Print out labels.

On the day: assemble the owl from the prepared parts. Cut out and stick on
the feathers and beak. Stick on white eye surrounds, then top with the googly
eyes. Secure the wings with split pins. Tape the ribbon hanger and the legs.
Stick the 'Wise sayings' sticker on the top lolly stick, then write your own wise
sayings on the remaining sticks. Secure the lolly stick sayings to the legs of
your owl with sticky tape.

Celebration

The sharing of recalled sayings and your chosen ones from Proverbs leads
naturally into reading Colossians 3:16 and conveying the message that God's
word is steadfast and revealed to us through Jesus.

Prayer

Faithful and steadfast God, we pray that your word dwells richly in our
hearts and that we share it with the same delight as we have enjoyed
this day recalling old sayings. Amen

Song suggestions

- When we walk with the Lord
- Thou, whose almighty word
- Immortal, invisible, God only wise
- At the name of Jesus
- Tell out my soul
- O worship the King

14

A time for everything

Bible passage

Ecclesiastes 3:1–8

Focus verse

> For everything there is a season,
>   a time for every activity under heaven
> ECCLESIASTES 3:1 (NLT)

Aim

To reassure everyone that God is in their every circumstance.

Messy team conversations

Talk about the seasons and how they influence what we do. Talk about gardening, orchards and trees, and the seasons for growing fruit, vegetables and flowers.

Activity

You will need: an A4 sheet of blue card for each person; brown funky foam or card; an assortment of shades of pink, cerise or white tissue paper; green tissue or other suitable border trim; small ready-made flowers or flower stickers; butterfly stickers; scissors; glue sticks or PVA glue and spreaders

In advance: out of the brown funky foam or card cut out two tree trunks per person and stick them on the blue A4 card (there's no need for the trunks to be the same).

On the day: turn winter into spring! Screw up small balls of tissue to create blossom and stick them on to the tree trunks. Cut a 30 cm strip of green border trim and secure it at the base. Add flowers and butterflies.

Celebration

Invite people to share what their favourite season is and why. Ask if anyone has special memories of activities associated with particular seasons, such as visits to the seaside, gathering blackberries or snowball fights.

Read Ecclesiastes 3:1–8. We cannot stop time and, as it rolls along, we all gather memories both happy and sad. Just as winter turns to spring, so too, when times feel dark for us, we have the hope and promise of God's faithfulness in every season of our lives.

Prayer

> Faithful God, we come to you with all of our joys and heartaches in the sure knowledge that, no matter what our circumstance, you are always there bringing hope and promise. Amen

Song suggestions

- Great is thy faithfulness
- The King of love my shepherd is
- Yes, God is good, in earth and sky
- The Lord is my shepherd
- For the beauty of the earth
- All things bright and beautiful

15

God remembers

Bible passage

Isaiah 49:13–16

Focus verses

'I will not forget you! See, I have engraved you on the palms of my
hands.'
ISAIAH 49:15–16 (NIV)

Aim

To remind us that God never forgets us, even though sometimes we may feel
that he has.

Messy team conversations

How do you remember things? Do you make a list? Put a note on the fridge?
Put a ring or watch on to the other hand? Write on your hand?

Activity

 **You will need: a copy of the poem template for each person;
pencils; crayons or felt-tip pens; paints; glitter (optional)**

In the space on the template, draw around one hand. Inside the hand print, ask each person to write words that describe themselves. Once they have done this, others who know them could contribute too – we are not always aware of our own strengths or talents, which other people may see!

Celebration

Look closely at our hands, the lines, the scars, the marks – what stories do they tell? Our hands are all different and unique.

Remember that each of us has a unique fingerprint too. Each of us is an individual and special to God our Father. Isaiah says that God knows our walls – our limitations, boundaries and difficulties.

Talk about jobs that we have done, such as parent, nurse, engineer, teacher, mechanic, cook, cleaner, shop assistant. What did we do with our hands?

If possible, have a model of praying hands. We can use our hands to bless and to pray. Spend some time reflecting on how God loves each of us.

Prayer

Loving Father God, thank you that you made each one of us. We are special and precious to you. You have promised never to leave us or forget us. Thank you for your endless love for us. Amen

Song suggestions

- He's got the whole world in his hands
- Thy hand, O God, has guided
- Amazing grace
- Father, I place into your hands
- Be still, for the presence of the Lord

16

The joy of the Lord

Bible passage

Isaiah 55:1, 3, 12

Focus verse

> You will go out in joy and be led forth in peace; the mountains and hills will burst into song before you, and all the trees of the field will clap their hands.
> ISAIAH 55:12 (NIV)

Aim

To share God's invitation to be blessed by him and thereby know abundant joy and peace.

Messy team conversations

Talk about trees and what they bring to us, e.g. shade, delight. If you were a tree, what sort would you be? What makes you burst with joy? Are rich people happier than those who are poor?

Activity

You will need: blue A4 card; brown tissue paper; green paper; bright wrapping paper, preferably with a fruit print; small paper flowers; green felt-tip pens or crayons; glue sticks or PVA glue and spreaders; 1 cm-wide double-sided tape; scissors

In advance: cut strips of green and patterned paper 2 cm wide and 10 cm long. You will need approximately 20 strips per person.

On the day: cut a tree trunk out of the brown tissue paper and stick it on to the blue card, leaving sufficient space at the bottom for a border. Cut a green border to represent hills and fields and secure it at the base of the tree. Make loops out of the green and coloured paper strips, securing them with double-sided tape. Arrange the loops on the tree, then stick them on using the glue sticks or double-sided tape.

Celebration

Share some of the table talk about bursting with joy, and discuss whether or not it's easier to be joyful in the western world than in poorer countries.

If facilities allow, show the clip of 'poor people praising God for the little they have' with great exuberance in their Malawian church (**youtube.com/watch?v=lhIIG1GDfPk**) or print off some pictures of people living in poverty praising God. What can we learn from people who have so very little? Does it help us to see things differently? We don't need wealth – we need God in our soul. Read the passage, before entering into enthusiastic praise!

Prayer

Gracious God, we thank you for your invitation to come and praise you with the same delight as the trees of the fields, for the freedom that you offer us, and for the joy and peace that knowing you brings. Amen

Song suggestions

- You shall go out with joy
- Give me joy in my heart
- Peace is flowing like a river
- Praise him, praise him, praise him in the morning
- For the beauty of the earth
- Praise, my soul, the king of heaven

17

Cracked pots

Bible passage

Jeremiah 18:1–6

Focus verse

'As the clay is in the potter's hands, so are you in my hand.'
JEREMIAH 18:6 (NLT)

Aim

To help people recognise that though we are all imperfect and may feel broken at times, God is waiting to restore us and has a plan for each and every person.

Messy team conversations

Talk about the variety of pots and vases there are. Think about their different uses. Could any one item be used for absolutely everything? What sort of pot do you most resemble?

Activity

 You will need: copies of pot templates 1 and 2 for each person, printed on heavy paper or thin card; coloured pencils; felt-tip pens; scissors; all-purpose glue; glue sticks

On template 1 create different patterns on each section of the pot using coloured pencils or felt-tips pens. Cut out the pot and each individual section to make a jigsaw. Re-assemble the 'cracked pot' on template 2 and stick the pieces down to form a new pot. Either each person could re-form their own pot or the jigsaws could be passed around, with the end product being given back to its owner.

Celebration

Read Jeremiah 18:1–6. While this passage is a warning of the impending destruction of the kingdom of Judah, the illustration that God gives to Jeremiah of the potter is a helpful reminder of God's faithfulness in our personal lives. We are all like 'cracked pots'. Each of us has our unique flaws and may feel broken and useless sometimes, yet God accepts us as we are, takes us is into his hands and moulds us to his purpose.

Share the story of the cracked pot, which you can download as a template. How has God reshaped us and used us in the past? Where do we share/show God's beauty?

Prayer

Creator God, as cracked pots we come to you today, trusting in your restoring hand and renewing grace. Amen

Song suggestions

- Spirit of the living God
- Take my life and let it be
- One more step along the world I go
- Praise to the Lord, the almighty
- Father, I place into your hands
- Great is thy faithfulness

18

No hiding place

Bible passage

Jonah 1:1–3

Focus verse

> [Jonah] bought a ticket… hoping to escape from the Lord.
> JONAH 1:3 (NLT)

Aim

To recognise that it is always better to ask for God's help to get through difficult situations rather than to run away from them.

Messy team conversations

Talk about sea journeys, either that people have made or famous ones. Has anyone sailed on rough seas? How did they feel?

Activity

You will need: 23 cm strong biodegradable paper plates; light and dark blue tissue paper; blue wool or string; coloured funky foam; PVA glue and spreaders; sticky tape; scissors; pencils

In advance: on one half of each plate, punch out 20 holes at regular intervals around the edge of the plate. Cut the tissue paper into small pieces roughly 2–3 cms – they don't all need to be the same. Cut out simple boat shapes from funky foam.

On the day: making sure that everyone is working with the holes on the bottom section of the plate, stick the dark blue paper squares to form the sea and the light blue ones to form the sky. Glue the boat into place. Draw some fish on funky foam, cut them out and stick them into place. Thread the wool or string through the holes to form the waves and secure the ends with sticky tape.

Celebration

Share some of the conversations that have taken place about sea journeys and introduce Jonah.

Read Jonah 3:1–3. Jonah wasn't going on holiday or on a great adventure; he was running away from God. Ask if anyone remembers what happens to Jonah when he tries to escape. Consider if we ever try to run away from God rather than face up to challenges with his help. Read Psalm 139:7–10 (NIV):

> Where can I go from your Spirit? Where can I flee from your presence? If I go up to the heavens, you are there; if I make my bed in the depths, you are there. If I rise on the wings of the dawn, if I settle on the far side of the sea, even there your hand will guide me, your right hand will hold me fast.

Prayer

> Eternal Father, whose right hand holds us fast, help us to journey with you through all the storms and challenges of our life. Amen

Song suggestions

- Lead us, heavenly Father, lead us
- Dear Lord and Father of mankind
- Great is thy faithfulness
- Lead, kindly light, amid the encircling gloom
- Through all the changing scenes of life
- When we walk with the Lord

NEW TESTAMENT

19

Let your light shine

Bible passage

Matthew 5:13–16

Focus verse

'Let your light shine before others, that they may see your good deeds and glorify your Father in heaven.'
MATTHEW 5:16 (NIV)

Aim

To help us all recognise ways in which the light of Jesus shines and reflects God's love through us.

Messy team conversations

Think about different sources of light. How do modern methods of lighting up your homes and streets differ from those in your childhood? How would it feel if you lived in darkness?

Activity

 You will need: a copy of the stained-glass template for each person to trace if they are able, or just one outline to be used for pre-preparation where necessary; tracing paper; black and coloured felt-tip pens or markers; rulers; coloured card; glue sticks; paper clips; a craft knife

In advance: cut the templates and the tracing paper to a 21 cm square. Make two frames per person by cutting the card into 21 cm squares and then, using a craft knife, cutting out a 16 cm square, leaving a 2.5 cm frame. If required, do the tracing for those of limited ability.

On the day: place the tracing paper over the outline and hold together with paper clips. Trace the picture using black felt-tip pens or markers, making sure that rulers are available. Colour in the picture on the tracing paper using coloured felt-tip pens. When complete, secure between two fames using glue sticks.

Celebration

Read Matthew 5:13–16. To see the true beauty of our pictures, we have to hold them up to the light. So too for our lives. For us to reflect the fullness of Jesus' love, we need to share the ways in which he shines his light through us, giving glory to God.

Share ways in which we can shine, from picking up a piece of rubbish off the street to making a phone call or preparing a banquet – and all things in between!

Prayer

Living Lord, by the power of your Holy Spirit may we feel the rays of your love shining in and through us, so that we may truly reflect God's glory. Amen

Song suggestions

- Lord, the light of your love is shining (Shine, Jesus, shine)
- This little light of mine
- Give me joy in my heart
- Lord Jesus Christ, you have come to us
- Make me a channel of your peace
- When we walk with the Lord

20

Messy jobs

Bible passage

Matthew 10:1, 5–10

Focus verses

'Go to the lost, confused people right here in the neighbourhood. Tell them that the kingdom is here.'
MATTHEW 10:6–7 (MSG)

Aim

To illustrate that Jesus calls ordinary people with all sorts of life and job skills to do his work.

Messy team conversations

When we look at the vast array of jobs that are mentioned in the Bible, we can find ourselves drawn more fully into the story, imagining or maybe identifying with the characters. Talk about jobs that people have done or dream jobs they would like to do. While being sensitive to possible issues, talk about retirement, unemployment and redundancy.

Activity

You will need: wooden spoons; funky foam; googly eyes; scraps of material; wool; lace; ribbon; buttons; sequins; all-purpose glue or glue sticks; double-sided sticky tape; red felt-tip pens

Make a 'selfie'. Using funky foam cut out two identical sets of clothes. Place the wooden spoon in the middle of one set and put the other set on top of the spoon to form the back and front of the outfit. Secure with double-sided sticky tape. Adorn as required: add wool hair and googly eyes and draw a mouth.

Celebration

Choose one of the following:

1 Think about jobs mentioned in the Bible – how many can people come up with? Encourage interactive conversation about past or present employment and think about discipleship within those roles. Conclude with reading and sharing thoughts on Matthew 10:1–10.

2 Take in some Happy Families playing cards. Share memories of playing the game and have fun looking at some of the jobs the families did. Could God use ordinary people like these? Read Matthew 10:1–10 and talk about the twelve disciples and other messy followers of Jesus.

Prayer

Loving Lord Jesus, you came to teach us the way to live and to love for the glory of God's kingdom. Help us to use our life and job skills to reach out to those around us in the same way. Amen

Song suggestions

- From heaven you came (The servant king)
- Take my life and let it be
- I want to walk with Jesus Christ
- Lord, you call us to your service
- Go, tell it on the mountain
- Go forth and tell! O church of God, awake

21

Treasures of the heart

Bible passage

Matthew 13:44–46

Focus verse

'Where your treasure is, there your heart will be also.'
MATTHEW 6:21 (NIV)

Aim

To discover, or rediscover, the most beautiful treasure of all.

Messy team conversations

Talk about everyone's treasured items. Share stories about what makes these items so special.

Activity

You will need: mini strong board boxes; scrapbook paper; quilling paper strips; PVA glue and spreaders; glue sticks; 1 cm-wide double-sided tape; scissors; quilling pens or any fine tool, such as mini kebab sticks; pencils; pearlescent beads for celebration

On the inside of a piece of scrapbook paper, draw around the lid of the box and cut out the shape. Cut a strip of paper the depth and circumference of the side of the box lid, and a further piece the depth and circumference of the side of the box. Assemble all the pieces on to the box and stick them into place, so that the whole box is covered. Using a quilling pen or other fine instrument, take a strip of quilling paper and tightly roll it around the tool until it is sufficiently tight to finish off by using your fingers. Continue to create the desired number of quills to form a pattern and stick them on to the box.

Celebration

Take in something of great value to you and share the treasured memory it evokes.

We all have wonderful things that we treasure here on earth, but the greatest treasure that we could ever obtain is heaven.

Read Matthew 13:44–46. To know Jesus as our Lord and Saviour is the most precious gift we will ever find. As Christians, we should be content not to hold on to and put first the things we own or do, but rather hold on to Jesus, who is the key to God's kingdom.

Give everyone a pearlescent bead to hold as you pray and afterwards allow a moment of quiet as they put the bead into their boxes.

Prayer

Lord, forsaking all else, may I know your presence in my heart to be the most precious treasure of all. Amen

Song suggestions

- Jesus, be the centre
- As the deer pants for the water
- Seek ye first the kingdom of God
- Be thou my vision
- Jesus calls us, o'er the tumult
- The kingdom of God is justice and joy

22

Seeing Jesus more clearly

Bible passage

Mark 8:22–25

Focus verse

Once more Jesus put his hands on the man's eyes. Then his eyes were opened, his sight was restored, and he saw everything clearly.

MARK 8:25 (NIV)

Aim

To help us see Jesus more clearly.

Messy team conversations

Encourage people to talk about how they view themselves – warts and all. Discuss how others may see them. Which famous people or places would people most like to meet or see?

Activity

You will need: pearlescent single-sided heavy A4 card cut in half to A5 size; funky foam; pencils; self-adhesive 13 mm mosaic mirror tiles; stickers; feathers; flowers; buttons; tissue; scissors; PVA glue and spreaders or glue sticks; thin ribbon; sticky tape

In advance: cut 9 cm funky foam squares and on them draw a frame of 16 small 1.5 cm squares on which to lay mirror tiles.

On the day: stick the self-adhesive mirror tiles into the frame and glue your completed foam square on to the card. Decorate with various materials. Make a loop of ribbon and attach it to the back of the card with sticky tape.

Celebration

Hold the completed craft projects up and discuss what people see. Our mirror view is slightly distorted; we need to look beyond that to appreciate the full picture. Show a picture (either projected or printed) of someone appearing to hold the Eiffel Tower or other well-known landmark. People and situations are not always as they appear. To see life in all its fullness, we need to ask Jesus to open our eyes.

Read Mark 8:22–25. The blind man came to healing gradually and with effort. Take in various strengths of inexpensive eyeglasses and ask for a volunteer, who has good vision, to put them on one at a time, starting with the strongest first. Ask them to describe what it feels like as vision becomes clearer.

Prayer

Jesus, we come to you as blind beggars and ask that you would lay your hands upon us and open our eyes. Take away our blemishes and faults, we pray, and enable us to see you more clearly. Amen

Song suggestions

- Be thou my vision
- Lord, the light of your love is shining (Shine, Jesus, shine)
- Come on and celebrate
- Open our eyes, Lord
- I am a new creation
- Come, let us sing of a wonderful love

23

New life in Jesus

Bible passage

Mark 9:2–8

Focus verse

> After six days Jesus… was transfigured before them.
> MARK 9:2 (NIV)

Aim

To recognise that God's timing is perfect in all the changing scenes of life.

Messy team conversations

Discuss how people feel about change: in lifestyle, family commitments, mobility, etc.

Activity

You will need: six jumbo lolly sticks (approx. 15 cm x 2 cm) per person; wide masking tape; small pom pom balls; narrow double-sided sticky tape; self-adhesive googly eyes; black pipe cleaners; felt-tip pens; scissors

In advance: prepare concertinas of six lolly sticks by taping together three pairs of two. When you have the three pairs completed, place the first pair face upwards, then add the second pair to it face down and tape them together.

Do the same with the third pair of lolly sticks. They should now fold into one. There are various YouTube clips if you experience difficulty.

On the day: run a strip of double-sided sticky tape across top stick of the concertina. Place pom poms on the tape and form a caterpillar, then complete with black pipe-cleaner antennae and googly eyes. Draw and colour in a butterfly on the remaining five sticks. If desired, do the same on the reverse. (Craft adapted from **daniellesplace.com**.)

Celebration

 Download the 'A life without colour' template and use it to illustrate the biblical passage.

Everything is in God's perfect timing, as was Jesus' transfiguration. The disciples will have struggled to take in and to understand what was unfolding before them, as indeed we do when things happen that will inevitably change our lives.

Prayer

Heavenly Father, we confess that we often struggle with change, but you reassure us that your timing is perfect and that you will transform our lives and situations if we simply place ourselves in your hands and listen to you. Amen

Offer a time of quiet reflection as you listen to a version of 'Be still'.

Song suggestions

- All heaven declares
- Lord, the light of your love is shining (Shine, Jesus, shine)
- Great is thy faithfulness
- Jesus, you are changing me
- Breathe on me, breath of God
- Immortal, invisible, God only wise

24

Letting go

Bible passage

Mark 10:17–27

Focus verse

> [The man] was holding on tight to a lot of things, and not about to let go.
> MARK 10:22 (MSG)

Aim

To help us all to let go of the burdens we carry and offload them to Jesus.

Messy team conversations

Has anyone seen or even ridden a camel? Talk about camels in biblical days being used to carry heavy goods over long journeys across the desert. Compare that with modern transport.

Activity

 You will need: background pictures of a narrow Jerusalem gate printed on A4 card; copies of the camel, coin and cup templates, printed on A4 card; coloured felt; coloured gems; bits of lace, ribbon and other scraps of suitable material; coloured pencils or felt-tip pens; scissors; PVA glue and spreaders

In advance: draw a simple camel or use the camel template to make a stencil for cutting out as many felt camels as are needed, keeping the scraps for people to cut out saddles and bags.

On the day: stick the felt camel on to the scene. Make a felt bag and decorate it with the gems. Stick the bag into place on the camel. Make a halter and saddle trim with lace and ribbon. Colour the coins and cups, then cut them out and load the bag.

Celebration

Look at the pictures created and talk about the impossibility of the camel getting in through that narrow gate. Explain that the only way in which camels carrying merchandise or rich person's wealth were able to do so was for them to be unloaded of everything and then, by going down on their knees, slowly getting through.

Read Mark 10:17–27. For us to enter into God's kingdom, we too have to let go of everything that's hindering us from doing so – not just material things that we may prize above God, but the luggage of life to which we often needlessly cling. It's not easy to lay all of our burdens down and it can be painful doing so, but by getting down on our knees and praying, Jesus will help us through.

Prayer

Thank you, Jesus, for always being there, ready to take my heavy load from me. Help me to be willing to let go of all that holds me back from trusting you and fully entering into the kingdom of God. Amen

Song suggestions

- All to Jesus I surrender
- What a friend we have in Jesus
- All I once held dear
- When we walk with the Lord

25

Bringing friends to Jesus

Bible passage

Luke 5:17–26

Focus verse

> Carry each other's burdens, and in this way you will fulfil the law of Christ.
> GALATIANS 6:2 (NIV)

Aim

To give people a tactile resource to use as an aid to prayer for their friends.

Messy team conversations

Encourage participants to choose a different coloured strand of wool for twelve different people and talk about their relationship with them and to think of themselves as the mat holding those people before Jesus.

Activity

You will need: plastic canvas sheets (size 7 mesh), cut into strips 12 holes wide by approx. 32 holes long (5 cm x 12 cm) – plastic canvas is available through most craft suppliers and online; twelve different coloured balls of wool; embroidery needles or plastic needles; scissors

Cut the wool into 20–22 cm lengths and weave through the plastic canvas to create a mat, leaving wool overhanging each end to form a tassel. Trim tassels to the same length.

Celebration

Tell the story from the paralysed man's perspective, whose only hope of getting to Jesus was through his friends. Can the people you have woven into your mat totally rely on you?

After brief thoughts on the biblical account, invite people to share one person's name aloud and then hold each of the other individual strands and silently pray for, or think about, each person they have woven into their mat. (You may wish to play a piece of gentle background music during this prayerful time.)

Encourage everyone to keep their 'prayer mat' as a reminder to pray regularly for the twelve people they have woven into it.

Prayer

Loving Lord Jesus, we lay at your feet our treasured friends. You know their needs and ours too. May they all know your abundant blessing, and may we be the supportive friends you would have us be. Amen

Song suggestions

- Father, I place into your hands
- What a friend we have in Jesus
- Kumbaya
- Brother, sister, let me serve you
- When I needed a neighbour

26

Messy neighbours

Bible passage

Luke 10:25–37

Focus verse

'Who is my neighbour?'
LUKE 10:29 (NIV)

Aim

To help us to think more deeply about who we consider our neighbour to be. Jesus makes it clear that everyone is. There are no boundaries or excuses for sharing God's love 24/7.

Messy team conversations

Talk about those who have been our geographical neighbours in the past and those with whom we share our lives now. Share thoughts on global neighbours.

Activity

You will need: household coil-sprung wooden clothes pegs, 7.5cm minimum; double-sided sticky tape; scissors; felt-tip pens; A4 thick card; craft wood glue

Twist the clothes peg and remove the spring. Reverse the two halves so that the long ends are back to back, then secure together with double-sided sticky tape. Draw each person present with felt-tip pens. Form into a circle with the lower third of each peg person firmly touching its neighbour. Take out one person at a time and secure it to its neighbour using wood glue. Cut a circle of thick card 15 cm in diameter (or appropriate to the size of your pegs) and glue it on to the back of the wooden peg circle for support. Decorate the card that shows through the gap in the middle of the circle of pegs.

Celebration

Share a personal experience illustrating neighbourly love or invite someone to come in and speak about a charity project which touches lives globally. Read the story of the good Samaritan (Luke 10:25–37) and think about how God calls us to love not only those with whom we happily rub shoulders but also those with whom we share no common ground.

Show one of the videos on **payitforwardday.com/inspire-me/inspiringvideos** or, If you have invited someone in to speak about a chosen charity, show their presentation.

Prayer

Jesus, our servant king, you came to show us how to love one another. Forgive us when we narrow that love to just our chosen few and help us to recognise that the circle of neighbours whom you ask us to serve is defined by your love, which knows no bounds. Amen

Song suggestions

- From heaven you came (The servant king)
- Bind us together, Lord
- A new commandment
- When I needed a neighbour
- Jesu, Jesu, fill us with your love
- He's got the whole world in his hands

27

Be still

Bible passage

Luke 10:38–42

Focus verse

'Be still, and know that I am God.'
PSALM 46:10 (NIV)

Aim

To encourage us not to get distracted from spending precious moments with Jesus.

Messy team conversations

Have lots of 'kitchen talk' – discuss favourite recipes; home baking versus bought; changes in appliances over the years; catering for guests; favourite gadgets and so much more!

Activity

You will need: air-dry clay; craft spatulas or glue spreaders; small pots of water

Please note: the coils mentioned in this activity are all attached to each other using the slip-and-score method. If you are not familiar with this method, there are many good instructions online.

Make the base of a pot by rolling out long coils of clay and swirling them into a circular shape, approximately 7 cm in diameter. Bind the base together. Take further pieces of clay and form them into smooth elongated coils approximately 24 cms in length. Use these to build the sides of the pot. Secure the first coil on to the base and trim off any excess length. Then continue adding coils, one on top of the other, until the desired size is achieved. Smooth the outside surface and use spatulas or glue spreaders to decorate.

Celebration

Share some of the 'kitchen talk' that has been taking place and think about the hours that some people have spent, and maybe still do spend, in the kitchen. Think too of other places in and around the home that hours are spent doing things, maybe in the garden or the garden shed. Ask how they would respond if someone special unexpectedly popped by. What if the visitor was Jesus?

Read Luke 10:38–42. Ask people to reflect on whether or not there are times when they, like Martha, have been distracted from being still and spending time with Jesus. Be still together and share a time of quiet at Jesus' feet.

Prayer

Loving Lord, as we still our hearts and minds, we come to you trusting that, in your mercy, you will forgive us for the times when we have been distracted and not made you our priority. Thank you, Father, for always being there, waiting for us. Amen

Song suggestions

- Be still, for the presence of the Lord
- Lord, I come to you
- Dear Lord and Father of mankind
- What a friend we have in Jesus
- O love that wilt not let me go
- Love divine, all loves excelling

28

A surprise invitation

Bible passage

Luke 19:1–10

Focus verse

[Jesus] said, 'Quick, come down! I must be a guest in your home today.'
LUKE 19:5 (NLT)

Aim

To encourage everyone to hand the invitation they have made to someone who would not normally participate in a Christian event.

Messy team conversations

Talk about sharing afternoon tea. What makes the occasion special? Discuss how people would feel if Jesus announced that he was coming to their home for tea. What would be your priority: the dust on the shelves or the state of your heart?

Activity

 You will need: copies of the afternoon tea templates; medium-weight A4 card; preprinted inserts; pens; scissors; glue sticks

Fold the A4 sheet in half. Cut out the required elements from the afternoon tea template and stick them on to the front of the card. Write a message on the inside to a friend, giving details of the Messy Vintage event to which you are inviting them, or have preprinted inserts ready to stick into the cards with space to write the person's name.

Celebration

Read Luke 19:1–10. Show people a teacup badly stained on the inside. Is it beyond saving or can it be cleansed? While recounting the story of Zacchaeus, soak the cup in a solution of water and steriliser (Milton Sterilising Fluid works quickly) and talk about the seemingly impossible being made possible. Invite people to think about the recipient of their Messy Vintage invitation, emphasising that even if it seems unlikely to them that the person will accept the invitation, Jesus may well have other ideas!

Prayer

Loving Lord Jesus, who seeks to save those who are lost, we earnestly pray that in the same way as you surprised Zacchaeus with an invitation that changed his life, so too would you stir the heart of the person into whose hands we will place our invitations. Amen

Song suggestions

- Come, let us sing of a wonderful love
- I, the Lord of sea and sky
- Lord, your church on earth is seeking
- Let us build a house (All are welcome)
- Give me the faith which can remove
- Go forth and tell! O church of God, awake

29

When the cock crows

Bible passage

Luke 22:32–34, 54–60

Focus verse

'I have prayed for you… that your faith may not fail.'
LUKE 22:32 (NIV)

Aim

To give thanks that Jesus prays that our faith will be strong and sure, even though he knows there are occasions when we let him down.

Messy team conversations

Ask if anyone has ever lived where the crow of a cockerel could be heard at daybreak. What was it like? Could you ignore it? Talk about other ways in which we can be called to rise early – alarm clocks, mobile alarms, someone giving you a shake. Ask if anyone can recall a cockerel crowing in a biblical account.

Activity

 You will need: copies of the cockerel template, printed on A4 card; coloured feathers; brightly coloured tissue paper, wrapping paper, foil, felt scraps or other suitable collage materials; buttons; coloured pencils or felt-tip pens; scissors; PVA glue and spreaders; ribbon hangers; sticky tape

Decorate the cockerel, giving him style and flamboyance.

Celebration

Give a brief overview of the last supper, then read Luke 22:32–34, 54–60. Invite people to share their thoughts on how Peter's denial would have made others feel. Share thoughts on how we sometimes deny Jesus without maybe realising the hurt it causes him and others – for example, when we don't acknowledge Jesus, when we don't live out what we profess to be or when we hurt people with unkind words.

Suggest to people that they may want to hang their cockerel picture some-where they can see it immediately as they wake up, to serve as a reminder that Jesus is praying that our faith will remain strong and sure throughout the day.

Prayer

Loving Lord, we thank you that, despite the way in which we sometimes deny you, you never deny us and you pray over us with an everlasting love. Amen

Song suggestions

- Dear Lord and Father of mankind
- Before the throne of God above
- May the mind of Christ my Saviour
- I need thee every hour
- God forgave my sins in Jesus' name
- Purify my heart

30

Born of the Spirit

Bible passage

John 3:1–8

Focus verse

> 'The wind blows wherever it pleases. You hear its sound, but you cannot tell where it comes from or where it is going. So it is with everyone born of the Spirit.'
>
> JOHN 3:8 (NIV)

Aim

To share the joy of having God's Spirit in our lives.

Messy team conversations

Take in pictures of dandelion seed heads and of dandelions in bloom, or better still the real thing. Ask if anyone remembers blowing a dandelion head and making a wish. Talk about wild flowers, thinking not only of their beauty but of how we view them, as weeds or beautifully created flowers.

Activity

You will need: sheets of A4 coloured card; eco-friendly cotton buds; green funky foam or green card; black funky foam or black card; scissors; glue sticks or PVA glue and spreaders

In advance: cut dandelion-shaped leaves out of the green funky foam or card, and 1 cm circles out of the black.

On the day: cut off one end of twelve cotton buds and cut four others in half. Create a flower head towards the top of the A4 card by sticking down the longer cotton bud pieces, with the cut ends touching each other in the centre. Overlay the halved pieces and some of the short cotton bud ends to create a 3D effect. Secure a little black circle in the centre. Cut out a stem and leaves using the green funky foam or card. Secure the stem under the flower head. Repeat the process to form a second, shorter flower head. Add the leaves. (Craft adapted from **craftymorning.com/pretty-dandelion-craft-ideas.**)

Celebration

Read John 3:1–8. Nicodemus was searching and wished dearly to know God more deeply, but he just could not understand that the answer came from himself – he needed to invite the Holy Spirit into his life to enable him to fully grasp the enormity of God's grace.

Just as the dandelion seed head lets go completely and lets God take over as its seeds are caught up by the wind to find a place to blossom and flourish, so too are we set free when we invite the Holy Spirit into our lives.

Prayer

Spirit of God, unseen as the wind, take over our lives that we may fully shine for you. Amen

Song suggestions

- Spirit of God, unseen as the wind (sung to the 'Skye Boat' tune)
- Breathe on me, breath of God
- Colours of day dawn into the mind
- Come down, O love divine
- The Spirit lives to set us free (Walk in the light)

31

Meeting Jesus
in unexpected places

Bible passage

John 4:6–15, 24–26

Focus verse

'I am speaking to you now.'
JOHN 4:26 (CEV)

Aim

To recognise that Jesus meets us in unexpected places and in unexpected ways.

Messy team conversations

Talk about life experiences, both good and bad. Encourage people to talk about their faith journey, both positive and challenging moments.

Activity

You will need: 14 cm square boards cut from MDF board or other strong material (we used offcuts of mounting board from a framing shop); mosaic stone tiles, available from Baker Ross; clear or aqua glass vase pebbles, available online or from most garden centres; strong adhesive

Stick the tiles on to the boards representing your faith journey or a particular time on your life journey. Somewhere on the board place one glass pebble representing a shining moment on your journey.

Celebration

Read John 4:3–42 or the shorter version, John 4:6–15, 24–26. Alternatively, if facilities allow, show the dramatised version 'Jesus and the Woman at the Well' (**youtu.be/sma4o3mCPwA**). Speak about how the woman at the well saw herself and how Jesus saw her. Talk about the places we expect to meet with Jesus. Where is our 'well'?

Prayer

> Loving Lord, forgive us when we fail to recognise that, though we are sinners, you wait for us in unexpected places to offer us your living water of eternal life. Amen

Song suggestions

- I stand amazed in the presence
- Blessed assurance
- I heard the voice of Jesus say
- Amazing grace
- And can it be that I should gain?

32

I am the gate

Bible passage

John 10:7–10

Focus verse

'I am the gate; whoever enters through me will be saved. They will come in and go out, and find pasture.'
JOHN 10:9 (NIV)

Aim

To share the glorious wonder of salvation.

Messy team conversations

Recall memories of playing hide-and-seek. Did anyone ever discover exciting new worlds as they sought out hidden corners? Talk about what the new world they would like to step into would look like.

If facilities permit, before commencing the craft show the two-minute clip from the film *The Chronicles of Narnia: The Lion, the Witch and the Wardrobe* when Lucy steps through the wardrobe and discovers a wonderful new world: **youtu.be/IO8v1yFoAwo**. Alternatively, read the relevant short passage from *The Lion, the Witch and the Wardrobe* by C.S. Lewis.

Activity

 You will need: a copy of the gate template for each person, printed on A4 card; paints; paint brushes; water pots; kitchen roll

Give everybody a copy of the template and invite them to paint the most beautiful scene they have ever beheld, or would most like to see, as they enter through the gate.

Celebration

Have a show-and-tell session of the lovingly created artwork, warts and all!

Talk about how the new world that Lucy entered was truly breathtaking, though not without problems. But good does ultimately conquer evil – albeit at a great cost, as Aslan gives up his life.

We too live in a troubled world and each of us goes through challenging and hard times of our own, but we have a Saviour – Jesus – and he has given his life for each one of us to enter into a breathtakingly beautiful new world. All we have to do is accept his invitation to enter. Read John 10:7–10.

Prayer

Good shepherd, we have not words enough to thank you for giving up your life to be the gate through which we enter into the most wondrous kingdom of all. To you be the honour and the glory, forever. Amen

Song suggestions

- To God be the glory, great things he hath done
- You laid aside your majesty
- I will enter his gates with thanksgiving in my heart
- Thank you, Jesus, thank you, Jesus
- And can it be that I should gain?
- I will sing the wondrous story

33

I am the good shepherd

Bible passage

John 10:14–16

Focus verse

'I have other sheep, too, that are not in this sheepfold. I must bring
them also. They will listen to my voice, and there will be one flock with
one shepherd.'
JOHN 10:16 (NLT)

Aim

To encourage the growth of Messy Vintage as an interdenominational, Christ-centred meeting place where all are welcome.

Messy team conversations

Which passages in the Bible menton sheep? Think about the role of a shepherd. Ask if anyone has seen sheep being herded. Are sheep all the same?

Activity

 You will need: copies of the sheep template; toilet rolls, preferably white; fluffy textured wool; heavy black paper; googly eyes; glue sticks or PVA glue and spreaders; scissors; lolly sticks; biros or fine felt-tip pens

Either supply each person with ready-cut face and limb parts or give out templates for people to cut out their own. Make a small slit in the top of the toilet roll and tuck the end of the wool in. Start wrapping the wool around until about two-thirds from the top is covered. Slide the top of each leg under the wool body and stick into place on the cardboard roll. Wrap wool around the top of the head shape. Add googly eyes and stick the finished head on to the body. Position the upper limbs and secure them into place. (Craft adapted from **redtedart.com/tp-roll-shaun-sheep-craft**.)

Celebration

Place some lolly sticks and pens on each table. Read John 10:14–16. Ask people what they like about being part of a Messy Vintage family. In the passage Jesus, the good shepherd, points out that not only does he know and care for each individual in his flock, but he also wants to gather more in, so that all may dwell together in his care. Ask people to think of friends and family whom they could invite to Messy Vintage, pointing out that Jesus, the good shepherd, isn't concerned about denomination or, indeed, whether these people have any faith at all. Rather, he is concerned about gathering people to him. Invite people to write the names of three or four people on lolly sticks, one name per stick, and then put the sticks into the sheep holders as you pray.

Prayer

Jesus, you are our good shepherd, the one who knows what is best for his flock. As we think about the great love you have for each one of us, help us to pray daily for the people whose names we have written down, so that they too may enter your Messy Vintage fold and experience for themselves your tender love and care. Amen

Song suggestions

- Father, I place into your hands
- Thy hand, O God, has guided
- The king of love my shepherd is
- The Lord's my shepherd
- How sweet the name of Jesus sounds

34

All you need is love

Bible passage

John 13:34–35

Focus verse

'Love one another. As I have loved you, so you must love one another.'
JOHN 13:34 (NIV)

Aim

To encourage us all to think more deeply on how we reflect the love of Jesus.

Messy team conversations

Talk about the many ways in which we show love. Discuss how we respond to people in our neighbourhood who may feel isolated, rejected, misunderstood or in need of help.

Activity

 You will need: an A4 sheet of white card per person with the focus verse written on the top; two large hearts per person, taken from template 1; eight small hearts per person, taken from template 2, ready cut out (or cut from red paper using a small heart die cutter) (optional); strips of coloured paper approx. 1 cm x 15 cm; glue sticks; 1 cm-wide double-sided tape; scissors; googly eyes; felt-tip pens

Cut out two large hearts and colour them in. If using template 2, colour in eight small hearts or give each person eight red die-cut hearts. Concertina-fold eight paper strips to create the arms and legs, then place all the elements on the A4 card to create little heart characters with arms and legs. Stick down the arms and legs with double-sided tape. Use the tape and additional glue to secure the large hearts over the top of the arms and legs for the body. Pop on googly eyes and draw a mouth. If using, stick the small hearts in place as hands and feet. (Craft adapted from **simplytodaylife.com/easy-valentines-day-heart-craft**.)

Celebration

Talk about Mother Teresa, who gave her life to working alongside the poorest of the poor, the utterly vulnerable and those who are totally rejected by society.

Prayer

Loving Jesus, help us to love others as you have loved us. May we reflect your love in everything we do, so that others see and meet Jesus through us. Amen

Song suggestions

- Make me a channel of your peace
- When I needed a neighbour, were you there?
- A new commandment I give unto you
- Jesu, Jesu, fill us with your love
- Jesus Christ is waiting, waiting in the streets
- Jesus' hands were kind hands, doing good to all

35

Jesus, the way, truth and life

Bible passage

John 14:1–7

Focus verse

'I am the way, the truth, and the life!'
JOHN 14:6 (CEV)

Aim

To help us see Jesus in every aspect of our lives, now and forever.

Messy team conversations

Talk about family, hobbies, holidays, interests, etc.

Activity

 You will need: cross templates, printed on white card; an A4 page of small pictures of hobbies, interests, church, people, landscape, architecture, etc. per person; all-purpose glue or glue sticks; scissors; laminator

Cut out the crosses and invite people to select pictures that represent their life story, then stick them on to the cross. Laminate and cut out the finished cross, leaving a small border to enable the lamination to remain secure.

Celebration

If available, bring in a María Gómez cross, or show a picture of one, portraying Maria's life working among the poor women of El Salvador. Tell María's story, then invite those gathered to share their life story as displayed on their cross.

Have a quiet time to allow people to fully enter into each picture that they have chosen to depict their journey. Draw the time to a close in prayer, allowing space for people to verbalise their prayers, should they so wish.

Prayer

Heavenly Father, we thank you that you are by our side every step of our journey, now and forevermore. Amen

Song suggestions

- All to Jesus I surrender
- Lord Jesus Christ, you have come to us
- From heaven you came (The servant king)
- When I survey the wondrous cross
- There is a green hill far away
- I know that my Redeemer lives
- Thine be the glory

36

Breakfast on the beach

Bible passage

John 21:1–10

Focus verse

> Early in the morning, Jesus stood on the shore, but the disciples did not realise that it was Jesus.
> JOHN 21:4 (NIV)

Aim

To help us remember that God is with us in good times and in bad and to encourage us to keep looking for him at work in our lives.

Messy team conversations

What are your memories of picnics, sausage sizzles, bonfires, eating fresh fish on the beach or having fish and chips wrapped in newspaper?

Activity

 You will need: fish templates; coloured card; pens; scissors; decorative scraps of material; wool; lace; buttons; bamboo canes; magnets; string; netting (e.g. from supermarket bags of fruit)

Using the templates, cut fish out of the coloured card. Decorate them, then write prayers on them and put them in the net. Make a fishing game by attaching small magnets to the card fish and writing on them some of the promises God has given us. Make fishing rods with bamboo canes, string and magnets. Take turns to catch fish and read out the promises.

Celebration

Read John 21:1–10. How were the disciples feeling? Think about times in our lives of failure, disappointment or great sadness. Jesus knows how we are feeling. He can work miracles and, amazingly, wants us to be part of his work!

The disciples initially didn't recognise Jesus, and it's often the same for us. How can we keep alert for God at work in our lives?

Prayer

> Loving Lord, thank you that you are with us in the sad and happy times of life, the successes and the failures. You know how we feel. Open our eyes and help us to see you at work in our lives and to listen for how we can play our part. Amen

Song suggestions

- Lord of the dance
- He's got the whole world in his hands
- Dear Lord and Father of mankind
- I am a new creation
- Be thou my vision

37

Grace and hope

Bible passage

2 Corinthians 12:7–10

Focus verse

'My grace is sufficient for you, for my power is made perfect in weakness.'
2 CORINTHIANS 12:9 (NIV)

Aim

To remind us to lean on Jesus and not trust in our own strength.

Messy team conversations

There is a story that an angel took pity on Eve as she and Adam were leaving the garden of Eden in winter as the snow was falling. Eve was crying, and the angel caught some snowflakes and turned them into snowdrops to comfort her and give her hope. Where are the best places to see snowdrops?

Activity

 You will need: snowdrop templates; 30 cm green pipe cleaners, cut in half; glue and glue sticks; green and white paper; green felt-tip pens; small jam jars

If possible, have some real snowdrop plants on the table to look at carefully. We will make them from paper.

Cut out thin green leaves (9 cm long and 3 cm wide at the middle) and green circles, 5 cm in diameter. Cut each one in half. Fold the white paper rectangle in half and open each half out. Fold the top corner to the middle crease. Then fold each side to the middle again. Snip across the top end and slide one end of the pipe cleaner into the white petal. Glue to secure.

Glue one side of the green paper semicircle and wrap it round the top of the flower. Fold the leaves in half lengthways and glue the bottom end to the bottom of the pipe cleaner. Arrange your finished flowers in a small jam jar. (Craft taken from **youtu.be/1CdEcnAV27w**.)

Celebration

Snowdrops look so delicate and fragile, but they survive harsh and freezing conditions and strong winds. We don't like feeling weak and helpless, but the apostle Paul says that in those times, God can work powerfully through us.

Listen quietly to a version of the hymn 'Amazing grace' and spend some time with God – give him your worries and weaknesses and ask for his strength to cope with each day.

Prayer

Strong and mighty God, when we feel weak, help us to rely on your strength. When we feel helpless, remind us of your mighty hand. When we feel lifeless, may you breathe your life into us. Thank you that you are our helper in times of weakness. Amen

Song suggestions

- Praise, my soul, the king of heaven
- Lord of all hopefulness
- What a friend we have in Jesus
- Give me joy in my heart
- Be still for the presence of the Lord

38

Live the fruit of the Spirit

Bible passage

Galatians 5:16–17, 22–26

Focus verses

> The fruit of the Spirit is love, joy, peace, patience, kindness, goodness, faithfulness, gentleness and self-control.
> GALATIANS 5:22–23 (NIV)

Aim

To encourage us to consider the fruit of the Spirit as a whole and work on those attributes we find more difficult.

Messy team conversations

Talk about likes and dislikes of the fruits as they are coloured in. Discuss what sort of fruit was most readily available to us as children and how it was consumed. Think about the smell of an apple pie cooking, about stirring strawberry jam, etc.

Activity

 You will need: eco-friendly 23 cm paper plates; 1 cm-wide double-sided tape; felt-tip pens; scissors; ribbon; sticky tape; copies of the fruit templates for each person

In advance: have ready a plate for each person, with a 12 cm circle cut out of the middle and strips of double-sided tape covering the remaining rim on the outside of the hole. Cut out the tags from the templates.

On the day: give each person a copy of the fruit templates to complete and cut out, then secure them on to the inside rim using the double-sided tape which has previously been attached. Hand out copies of the fruit of the Spirit words and cut out them out. Secure them around the fruit. Add the 'Live the fruit of the Spirit' tag. Secure a hanger of ribbon on to the back of the finished craft. (Craft adapted from **wisconsinumc.org**.)

Celebration

Ask which fruit people would most liken themselves to and why. Then ask them to imagine themselves as a mixture of all – a fruit salad containing everything. How would they feel?

Read Galatians 5:16–17, 22–26. Explain that we cannot choose just some of the fruit of the Spirit; we need to strive to achieve them all, even the attributes we find difficult.

Prayer

Loving Lord, help us to lay aside our sinful nature and live the fruit of the Spirit in all of its richness. Amen

Song suggestions

- Come down, O love divine
- Spirit of God, unseen as the wind
- Breathe on me, breath of God
- There's a spirit in the air
- O breath of life, come sweeping through us

39

Rooted and grounded

Bible passage

Ephesians 3:16–19

Focus verses

> And I pray that you, being rooted and established in love, may have power, together with all the Lord's holy people, to grasp how wide and long and high and deep is the love of Christ.
>
> EPHESIANS 3:17–18 (NIV)

Aim

To encourage and remind us to keep close to Jesus.

Messy team conversations

If you have trees in view, look at them. If not, bring along pictures of different trees. Talk about childhood activities involving trees – climbing, lying under a summer tree and looking up at the sky, kicking autumn leaves, etc. What's your favourite type of tree and why?

Activity

You will need: brown or green pipe cleaners; tissue paper of different colours; glue and glue sticks; small plastic pots; air drying clay; sand; small stones

Taking five pipe cleaners each and twist them together in the middle, leaving 8 cm at one end and 5 cm at the other. Press the shorter ends into the clay in the small plastic pot. Spread out the longer ends into 'branches' and arrange into a tree shape – bonsai, willow, etc. Attach strips of coloured tissue paper with the glue to the branches to make leaves, fruit, flowers, birds' nests, etc. Cover the clay and the 'roots' in sand and then add small stones on top to finish.

Celebration

Trees are mentioned a lot in the Bible – especially in Genesis and in the gospels. How many mentions can you think of?

Read Psalm 1 and Ephesians 3:16–19. Think about our roots, leaves and fruit. Are we a shelter and a shade? What do we need to be doing to stay rooted and grounded in Jesus?

Prayer

We praise and thank you, God, for your great love for us. Help us to take it in and to continue to grow deeper into you, keeping close to Jesus. Help us to 'stay green and to yield fruit for you'. Amen

Song suggestions

- He's got the whole world in his hands
- Great is thy faithfulness
- Praise, my soul, the king of heaven
- 10,000 reasons (Bless the Lord, O my soul)
- You shall go out with joy

FESTIVALS

40

Advent

Bible passage

Isaiah 40:3–5

Focus verse

'In the wilderness prepare the way of the Lord, make straight in the desert a highway for our God.'
ISAIAH 40:3 (NRSV)

Aim

To prepare our hearts for the coming of Christ at Christmas.

Messy team conversations

What did you do as a child in the weeks before Christmas? How did you prepare? Did you stir the Christmas pudding on Stir-up Sunday? Did you make Advent wreaths? Talk about the four candles, one for each Sunday in Advent, three purple and one pink – for the third Sunday in Advent.

Activity

You will need: OASIS floral foam or polystyrene foam rings sitting on a base, e.g. a plate or board; water in a bowl; cocktail sticks; greenery, preferably from a natural evergreen, e.g. conifer, hebe, ivy, pittosporum, yew, rosemary or euonymus, but something artificial can also be used; LED tea lights or small pillar candles, ideally three purple and one rose-coloured; pine cones sprayed gold; ribbon; small baubles

If using OASIS foam, soak it in water. Mark where the four candles will go with the cocktail sticks, spaced evenly around the ring. Insert foliage, using the larger pieces for the base and smaller pieces at the sides and into the middle, being careful not to fill up the middle. Secure the candles with candle holders or, if using LED tea lights, place them on the ring, tucked in among the foliage, so that you can lift them up to switch them on and off. Add ribbon, pine cones or small baubles as wished.

Celebration

Share what you've been talking about with regards to traditions and customs of preparing for Advent.

Advent is a time of waiting, but also of action. Reviewing our actions and attitudes, does anything need changing? Spend some time with Jesus, asking him to help us prepare – for the king who has come, is still coming and will come again.

Prayer

Father, Son and Holy Spirit, as we spend Advent waiting for you, bless us with the knowledge of your presence. Amen

Song suggestions

- Make way, make way
- Open our eyes, Lord
- Restore, O Lord
- Tell out my soul
- Make me a channel of your peace

41

Christmas

Bible passage

Luke 2:8–14

Focus verse

> The angel said to them, 'Do not be afraid; for see – I am bringing you good news of great joy for all the people: to you is born this day in the city of David a Saviour, who is the Messiah, the Lord.'
> LUKE 2:10 (NRSV)

Aim

To celebrate the coming of the Christ-child and to remember the message of the angels, 'Do not be afraid.'

Messy team conversations

Have you ever seen a real angel? How did you know? Do you think they always have white wings and a halo? Do you know any earthly 'angels'? If you are able to, listen to 'Angels' by Robbie Williams.

Activity

You will need: pine cones of different sizes; white or gold feathers; small polystyrene balls; self-adhesive googly eyes; felt-tip pens; glue and glue sticks; ribbon or pretty cord; gold sparkly pipe cleaners; scissors

Hold the pine cone so that the wider part is at the bottom. Wrap the cord or ribbon in a loop around the pine cone so that you can hang it on a tree. On to the polystyrene ball, stick or draw two eyes and then draw a nose and smile to make the head. Cut a small piece of sparkly pipe cleaner and glue it on to the head as a halo. Glue the head on top of the pine cone. Fix feathers on to the back of the pine cone, ideally two sets but at least one each side as wings. Continue until you have a host of heavenly angels! (Craft adapted from **peacebutnotquiet.com/pinecone-angels.**)

Celebration

Angels are scary people – perhaps that's why they always start by saying 'Do not be afraid!' But they mean it – the love of God is always stronger than our fear.

Spend some time giving God our fears and worries. If possible, listen to 'The angel's carol' by John Rutter or 'Angels (Singing Gloria)' by Matt Redman, and enjoy time with God, thanking him for sending Jesus to us.

Prayer

Loving God, we thank you for your great love for us, so great that you sent your beloved Son as a vulnerable baby. Help us this Christmas time to hear the angel's message and to know that you are with us. Amen

Song suggestions

- Angels from the realms of glory
- While shepherds watched their flocks by night
- Away in a manger
- Once in royal David's city
- Infant holy, infant lowly

42

Epiphany

Bible passage

Matthew 2:1–12

Focus verse

> On entering the house, they saw the child with Mary his mother; and
> they knelt down and paid him homage. Then, opening their treasure-
> chests, they offered him gifts of gold, frankincense and myrrh.
> MATTHEW 2:11 (NRSV)

Aim

To help us refocus on Jesus at the start of the new year and give our hearts
to him afresh.

Messy team conversations

What travels did you do in your younger days? Journeys to see relatives,
journeys of discovery? What special gifts do you remember?

Activity

 **You will need: a large (around 30 cm diameter) or individual
smaller metal rings (e.g. made from metal coat hangers
or floristry rings); gold card; scissors; a copy of the camel
template for each person; brown felt or cardboard; self-
adhesive googly eyes; decorative jewels; a stapler; thread or**

**string; items to represent the gifts from the Magi (see below); a
heart-shaped card for each person; pens; ribbon; a hole punch**

Create a mobile with the following items on it:

- a large star cut from the gold card
- three camels of felt or cardboard (use the template), with googly eyes
  attached
- a gold crown cut out of gold card and decorated with jewels. Staple it into
  a circle and secure with thread through two opposite points
- items to represent the gifts from the Magi (e.g. a small gold box, a small
  net bag containing little pebbles, a felt shape)
- a card heart for each person to write their names on and a prayer.

Connect each item with ribbon to the central ring, and suspend the mobile
with more ribbons in an open space where it can move.

Celebration

Thinking about the new year ahead, what is most important? Read Matthew
2:1–12. Read verse 1 of the poem 'The gate of the year', by Minnie Louise
Haskins. If possible, listen quietly to 'In the bleak midwinter' and reflect on
the words of the last verse. How can we give our hearts to Jesus? What can
we do to follow him in the coming days?

Prayer

Lord Jesus, you are with us every step of our lives, as you were with the
Magi. Please guide us and sustain us on our own journeys, so that we
might safely reach the destination with our eyes fixed on you. Amen

Song suggestions

- We three kings of Orient are
- Brightest and best of the sons of the morning
- Hills of the north, rejoice
- One more step along the world I go
- Lord of the dance

43

Candlemas (February)

Bible passage

Luke 2:22–32, 36–38

Focus verse

'A light for revelation to the Gentiles and for your glory to your people Israel.'
LUKE 2:32 (NRSV)

Aim

To celebrate Jesus as light of the world.

Messy team conversations

This passage is about old people, waiting patiently, faithful in prayer and trusting God – and they were rewarded with a sudden moment of recognition and joy. Chat about those moments when you have had flashes of understanding and about the things that you have been patiently waiting for, perhaps for years.

Activity

You will need: clean jam jars, one for each person; LED tea lights; acrylic pens or glass paint; tissue paper; glue and glue sticks; double-sided sticky tape; patterned tape; lace and ribbon

Decorate the jam jars as you wish, and put an LED tea light in each one.

Celebration

Read Luke 2:22–32, 36–38. Light your tea lights and thank God for Jesus, the light of the world.

If possible, listen to a version of the Nunc Dimittis (the song of Simeon).

Prayer

Light of the world, thank you that you use us to spread your good news, just as you spoke through Anna and Simeon, and that we are included in your salvation plan. May you reveal more of yourself to us day by day. Amen

Song suggestions

- Christ, be our light
- Let the flame burn brighter (We'll walk the land)
- This little light of mine
- Lord, the light of your love is shining (Shine, Jesus, shine)
- Light of the world, you stepped down into darkness

44

Lent

Bible passage

Matthew 4:1–4

Focus verse

'One does not live by bread alone, but by every word that comes from the mouth of God.'
MATTHEW 4:4 (NRSV)

Aim

To help us keep close to Jesus and remember that Jesus understands our doubts and knows our hard times.

Messy team conversations

Chat about Lent traditions – what did you give up? Or take on? What temptations have you faced? Have you made your own bread? The smell and taste are irresistible – especially if you are really hungry.

Activity

You will need: baking mats or plates to work on; bread dough; a knife for cutting; a baking tray; poly bags to take the rolls home in

In advance: make a batch of bread dough, sufficient for each person to have approximately 170 g each. This will make two or three rolls. You may wish to bring some baked rolls to eat with butter during your refreshment time.

On the day: spend time kneading the dough, then cut it into pieces and shape the pieces into rolls – plaits or rounds. Arrange on the baking trays and cook for 15–20 minutes while you have the celebration. Think about the process of making bread: waiting for the yeast to work, allowing it to rise in the warmth, knocking it back and shaping and moulding it. It takes time to make bread, as it takes time for God to work in and through us. Often it's in the hard times that we learn and grow the most.

Celebration

If possible, display an image of the painting *Christ in the Desert* by Ivan Kramskoi, reflecting the temptations that Jesus experienced. How do you think Jesus feels there?

Life is not easy. We all go through hard times – failure, rejection, disappointment, loss. We can be sure that Jesus knows what we are going through, as he has been there too. He has promised never to leave us. Spend some time talking to God about the hard times in your life and thanking him for his help.

Prayer

> Thanks be to thee, my Lord Jesus Christ,
> for all the benefits thou hast given me,
> for all the pains and insults which thou hast borne for me.
> O most merciful redeemer, friend and brother,
> may I know thee more clearly, love thee more dearly
> and follow thee more nearly, day by day. Amen
> St Richard of Chichester (1197–1253)

Song suggestions

- Father, hear the prayer we offer
- Lead us, heavenly Father, lead us
- Give thanks with a grateful heart
- Spirit of the Living God, fall afresh on me
- What a friend we have in Jesus

45

Palm Sunday

Bible passage

Matthew 21:1–11

Focus verse

A very large crowd spread their cloaks on the road, while others cut branches from the trees and spread them on the road.
MATTHEW 21:8 (NIV)

Aim

To remember and reflect on the hopes and expectations on that first Palm Sunday.

Messy team conversations

Chat about donkeys – have you ever ridden on one? Have you taken part in a Palm Sunday procession?

Activity

You will need: palm leaves or strips of paper, 1–3 cm inches in width and 35–40 cm long; scissors; crayons or felt-tip pens; stickers or gems to decorate (optional)

Make palm crosses and then decorate them how you wish. The team should familiarise themselves with a good YouTube instruction video and have plenty of practice beforehand, so that you will be able to teach on the day of the session. (For this activity, there are several good YouTube videos on the internet, including Building Faith CMT and faithatstb.)

Celebration

Read Matthew 21:1–11. Everyone had different expectations on that first Palm Sunday procession into Jerusalem: the crowd wanted freedom from Roman oppression, the disciples wanted power, the Jewish religious leaders wanted things to stay the same. What are your hopes and expectations? What can you give to Jesus?

Prayer

'Hosanna to the Son of David!'
Jesus, we praise you for saving us.

'Blessed is he who comes in the name of the Lord!'
Jesus, thank you that you are the perfect king.

'Hosanna in the highest heaven!'
Jesus, we give you all the glory. Amen

Song suggestions

- Make way, make way
- Meekness and majesty
- Lord of the dance
- All glory, laud and honour
- Give me joy in my heart, keep me praising

46

Easter

Bible passage

John 20:11–17

Focus verse

> Jesus said to her, 'Mary.'
> JOHN 20:16 (NIV)

Aim

To remind us of Mary's joy in that first Easter garden and that Jesus calls each of us by our name.

Messy team conversations

Chat about gardens – your own or those you have visited. Think about favourite plants and trees, and the most peaceful gardens. There is a saying, 'You're nearer to God in a garden than anywhere else on earth.' Do you think that's true?

Activity

You will need: trays; small flowerpots for the cave; small stones; soil; small plants; moss; large stones to cover the entrance of the cave; small sticks or lolly sticks; string; small pieces of white cloth

Make an Easter garden, either a large one or small individual ones. Place the flowerpot on its side at the edge of the tray and cover it with moss or soil. Place the three crosses (sticks tied with string) into the soil behind it. Place the white cloth folded inside the 'tomb' and put the large stone to the side of the entrance. Cover the rest of the tray with soil, a stone path, flowers, moss, etc. as wished.

Celebration

Gardens are mentioned several times in the Bible. For example, Jesus prayed in the garden of Gethsemane before his arrest.

Read John 20:11–17. Imagine Jesus standing in front of you and saying your name. Take a few moments to enjoy being with Jesus.

Prayer

Risen Christ, we praise you and thank you for giving yourself for us. Help us to hear your voice and know that you love us. Amen

Song suggestions

- This is the day
- I am a new creation
- Thine be the glory
- Alleluia, alleluia, give thanks to the risen Lord
- The head that once was crowned with thorns

47

Rogationtide (May)

Bible passage

Deuteronomy 8:6–10

Focus verse

You shall eat your fill and bless the Lord your God for the good land that he has given you.
DEUTERONOMY 8:10 (NRSV)

Aim

To praise God for his beautiful world and take action to look after it.

Messy team conversations

Rogationtide is celebrated on the three weekdays before Ascension Day. It's a time when we ask God's blessing on the land and crops. Often there was a procession around the parish boundary – 'beating the bounds' – to pray for a good harvest. Chat about memories of traditions around Rogation or Plough Sunday (in January). What can you do to look after creation?

Activity

You will need: a square piece of wood (approx. 30 x 30 cm) per person; two thin pieces of wood per person; three clean, empty tin cans per person; wood glue; hollow bamboo canes; non-toxic PVA glue; glue sticks; paint and paintbrushes

Bees are vital in the process of pollination, but numbers are in decline. (Thanks to World Wildlife Fund for this craft, which may be found at **wwf. org.uk/sites/default/files/2019-04/WWF_Bee_Hotel_Activity_Sheet.pdf**).

Make a bee hotel. Place the square piece of wood on a flat surface and glue the bottom of the cans to the wood in a pyramid shape (two below, one on top). Leave to dry. Take the two thin pieces of wood and place them in a triangle shape to form a roof for the cans. Glue in place and leave to dry.

Cut the bamboo canes into short sections which fit into the depth of the tin cans. Place a little PVA glue on the end of each cane and push it into the can. Fill up each can with canes. Paint the bee hotel in bright colours with non-toxic paint and leave it in a quiet, sunny place outside.

Celebration

If possible, read the poem 'God's grandeur' by Gerard Manley Hopkins. Read Deuteronomy 8:6–10. Praise God for his creation and his faithfulness.

Prayer

> God of nature, who has blessed the work of our hands, we pray that you would make us good stewards of your gifts. Help us to provide for those who have less than we do and to share all the good things you give us. Amen

Song suggestions

- Praise, my soul, the king of heaven
- Praise God from whom all blessings flow
- All things bright and beautiful
- Great is thy faithfulness
- How great thou art

48

Pentecost

Bible passage

Acts 2:1–4

Focus verse

All of them were filled with the Holy Spirit and began to speak in other tongues as the Spirit enabled them.
ACTS 2:4 (NIV)

Aim

To celebrate the gift of the Holy Spirit given at the first Pentecost and how she works in and through us today.

Messy team conversations

Pentecost used to be called Whit Sunday. Did you have any traditions or activities on that day?

Activity

 You will need: a laminating machine; A4 laminating pouches; tissue paper in lots of different colours but especially red, orange and yellow; dove template on white paper; 5 cm circles cut out from gold paper; 20 cm diameter plates; pens; scissors; a hole punch; ribbon

Turn the laminator on to heat up. Open the pouches and, on the bottom sheet, arrange strips of torn tissue paper in different colours to look like flames. In the middle, arrange the dove and put the gold halo under its head. Carefully close the pouch, ensuring that there are no bits of tissue paper sticking out at the sides and that the dove and halo stay in the same place. Carefully feed the pouch into the laminator (folded end first). Lay the laminated picture flat and place the plate upside down on it, ensuring that the dove remains central and pointing downwards. Draw around the plate and cut out the circle. Ensuring that the dove is still directing downwards, make a hole in the top of the sun-catcher and thread a ribbon through it.

Celebration

If possible, hang the Pentecost sun-catchers by a window so the light shines through them.

Read Acts 2:1–4. I wonder what it felt like to be in that room, on that day. Ask God to send his Holy Spirit to us by singing or saying the words of 'Spirit of the living God, fall afresh on me'.

Prayer

Holy Spirit, sent by the Father, ignite in us your holy fire; strengthen your children with the gift of faith, revive your church with the breath of love, and renew the face of the earth, through Jesus Christ our Lord. Amen

Song suggestions

- Be still for the presence of the Lord
- The Spirit lives to set us free
- Breathe on me, breath of God
- How great thou art
- Love divine, all loves excelling

49

Sea Sunday (July)

Bible passage

Acts 27:18–25

Focus verse

'So keep up your courage.'
ACTS 27:25 (NIV)

Aim

To remember to trust God during storms in our lives. To think about those who live and work on the sea, transporting goods and passengers, and the chaplains who serve them.

Messy team conversations

Chat about journeys on ships, holidays, travel to see family. Have you been sailing? Do you get seasick?

Activity

You will need: 50 g wool in bright colours (double knit or four-ply); size 8 needles (4 mm); large eye needles; scissors

Knit hats for the Mission to Seafarers, who can distribute them to sailors who need them. This activity may be started during the session and completed for the next session.

Pattern
- Cast on 120 stitches. Knit rib (two plain, two purl) for 30 cm.
- Next row: knit two together to the end of the row (60 stitches).
- Next row: purl. Repeat the last two rows (30 stitches).
- Next row: knit.
- Next row: purl.

Pull the thread through all the stitches and sew up the seam. Details of where to send the finished articles can be found at **missiontoseafarers.org**.

Celebration

Praise God for the seas and all that lives in them. Pray for fishermen, the RNLI and the coastguard, the Mission to Seafarers and the Sailors' Society. Pray too for refugees undertaking dangerous crossings.

Prayer

Lord God, creator of land and sea, bless those who work at sea. Be with them in good weather and bad. Protect them and keep them safe. Give them strength and comfort when they are tired and far away from their homes and families. Help us to look after the oceans and all the fish and the creatures who live there. Amen

Song suggestions

- Eternal Father, strong to save
- In Christ alone
- Be thou my vision
- My Jesus, my Saviour
- My lighthouse

50

Harvest

Bible passage

Mark 4:26–29

Focus verse

The Lord keeps watch over you as you come and go, both now and forever.

PSALM 121:8 (NLT)

Aim

To think about the many ways in which God has watched over us from childhood, even though we are often unaware of his presence.

Messy team conversations

Talk about childhood memories. Encourage sharing of life experiences, family, work and hobbies.

Activity

You will need: thin garden canes; green garden tape; polystyrene balls; cupcake cases; wool; self-adhesive googly eyes; peppercorns; raffia; material; ribbon; funky foam or material scraps; scissors; double-sided sticky tape or glue stick; sticky tape; red pen

With two pieces of garden cane, form a cross approx. 30 x 22 cm and secure
it with green garden tape or sticky tape. Cut a piece of material 50 cm x 20
cm and double it over. Cut a small hole in the top centre and place it over the
stick. Place a polystyrene ball on top and construct the head, securing hair
(wool) and hat (cupcake case) with double-sided tape or a glue stick. Stick
on the eyes and make a peppercorn nose and draw on the mouth. Make raffia hands and secure on to the ends of the horizontal stick with sticky tape.
Decorate the tunic with scraps of foam or material. Add a ribbon tie and a
raffia belt.

Celebration

Take in a half-grown seedling and talk about what it has come from, what it
might become and how it needs nurturing throughout its existence.

Draw attention to the cross underneath the scarecrow's clothing and think
about the way God watches over us as we grow and flourish. You may wish
to give a personal account of a time when you have felt particularly watched
over and protected.

Read Mark 4:26–29, the parable of the growing seed. Remind people of God's
ever-present love for each and every one of us.

Prayer

Creator God, we thank you for walking with us through every season
of our lives, nurturing and growing us even when we are unaware of
your presence. Amen

Song suggestions

- Now thank we all our God
- Great is thy faithfulness
- We plough the fields and scatter
- For the fruits of his creation
- Love divine, all loves excelling

51

Bible Sunday (October)

Bible passage

Proverbs 3:5–6

Focus verse

> Trust in the Lord with all your heart, and do not rely on your own insight.
> PROVERBS 3:5 (NRSV)

Aim

To help us go deeper with scripture.

Messy team conversations

Start with prayer. Ask God to open your eyes, ears and hearts to this scripture. There may not be much conversation with this activity!

Activity

You will need: copies of the verses on paper (A4 or A5 size); extra paper; coloured pencils or felt-tip pens; highlighters; decorations, such as stickers, washi tapes, decorative stamps, etc.

Bible journalling is a way of engaging deeper with the Bible. Encourage everyone to read and reflect on the passage. How does this verse apply to you and your life? Are there particular words that jump out at you? How do you see them? Underlined? Highlighted? Coloured differently? Be creative!

If you wish, plan your drawing on a separate piece of paper first, then draw up your final version once you're happy with it.

If you liked this activity, there is a lot of information about Bible journalling on the internet, and there are dedicated journalling Bibles available to buy.

Celebration

You might like to download/send off for some information from the Bible Society about their work.

There are lots of verses in the Bible about God's word – can you think of some? Read Psalm 119:105 and Proverbs 3:5.

Thank God for his word. Pray for the work of Bible Society, The Bible Reading Fellowship and all who work to enable everyone to read God's word.

Prayer

> Blessed Lord, thank you for your word recorded for us in scripture. Help us to read it with our hearts open to your Spirit, that we may find comfort and life in its pages. Thank you that your living Word, Jesus, is alive and reigns with you. Amen

Song suggestions

- All my hope on God is founded
- Lord, for the years
- May the mind of Christ my Saviour
- Seek ye first the kingdom of God
- Thou, whose almighty word

52

All Saints' Day (November)

Bible passage

Ephesians 6:13–17

Focus verse

> In addition to all this, take up the shield of faith, with which you can
> extinguish all the flaming arrows of the evil one.
> EPHESIANS 6:16 (NIV)

Aim

To encourage us in our struggles.

Messy team conversations

Tell the story of a favourite saint, perhaps the story of St George and the
dragon. But there is another story – the real St George wasn't English; he
was born in Palestine and brought up a Christian. He was a soldier in the
Roman army. In 303, the emperor ordered that every Christian in the army
should be arrested. George objected, publicly declared himself a Christian
and renounced the emperor's decision. In spite of attempts to dissuade him,
George stood firm and was beheaded on 23 April 303.

Activity

 You will need: some examples of heraldic shields and their
meanings; a copy of the shield templates, printed on A4 card
for each person; pencils, felt-tip pens, watercolours or paints;

spare paper to plan; copies of plant catalogues or magazines; silver foil; glue and glue sticks

Heraldry in days gone by was about using your shield to tell people who you are and what you are like. Bright colours were used, and pictures of all kinds to symbolise different things. The stag symbolised wisdom and long life; the badger, endurance; a dog, faithfulness. All kinds of fruit were considered to be symbols of God's kindness and goodness. The bee was a symbol of industry, creativity, diligence and wealth.

As you create your own shield, think about what will go on it – what is important to you? What are your values?

Celebration

Share the stories of your shields. Spend time praising God for all he has given us and pray for courage to be a true witness to Jesus. The apostle Paul exhorts us to 'always keep on praying for all the Lord's people' (Ephesians 6:18, NIV).

Pray for each other and ourselves, and for those who are persecuted, imprisoned or killed for their faith. You may wish to find out about an organisation that supports people in these situations, e.g. Open Doors.

Prayer

Lord of all history, the saints throughout the ages proclaim your name. Teach us through the stories of your followers, past and present, to draw closer to you with joy. Amen

Song suggestions

- When a knight won his spurs
- Stand up, stand up for Jesus
- Lord, for the years
- When the saints go marching in
- For all the saints

Appendix I

Memorandum of understanding for care homes

Thank you for inviting the Messy Vintage team to come into your care home on a monthly basis to lead a creative, celebratory, biblical-based session with residents.

The sessions will last one-and-a-half to two hours and we welcome any family members and staff who would like to join in with us and your residents. Each of the team will wear a name badge and will sign in/out and follow any safety instructions given by your staff.

Our team are:

Names: ....

....

....

All of us have completed safeguarding training.

Dates: ....

....

....

In order to provide a successful Messy Vintage session, we need:

- A suitable space for the Messy Vintage session to take place
- A member of the care staff or the activity coordinators to be there during the sessions
- To join you for the afternoon tea at the end of the session
- Your feedback after the session as to how it went and what needed to change or improve, if anything
- Consent for us to take photos of the activities and your staff and residents during the Messy Vintage sessions
- Help with gaining feedback from the residents about the sessions
- Information on your fire safety procedures.

We will:

- Keep in touch regarding the dates and activities, make changes as required and provide a poster to advertise the session in the home on the week before it takes place
- Provide all the materials needed
- Set up before the session and clear away afterwards.

Thank you for your support for this new venture! We hope your residents and staff enjoy it, and we look forward to working with you.

If you would like to get in touch, your Messy Vintage team leader is:

Name: ....

Tel: ....

Email: ....

This appendix is available to download at **messychurch.org.uk/ messy-vintage**.

Appendix II

Volunteer role guidance: Messy Vintage team member

Thank you very much for your interest in volunteering to help with Messy Vintage.

Messy Vintage is Christ-centred, creative, celebratory worship with older people, based on a Bible story or passage with songs, prayers and refreshments, lasting between one-and-a-half and two hours. It may be held in a care home, a church or community hall or some other accessible space.

What is essential for the role

- A love of Jesus Christ and a desire to share your faith with older people through actions and words
- Being a good listener
- A positive, cooperative, helpful, loving attitude to the members of the team and all older people
- An understanding that it's messy and will never be perfect!
- An up-to-date DBS certificate as required by your denomination
- Safeguarding training completed as required by your denomination.

The role includes

- Praying for the Messy Vintage sessions, guests and team, for sufficient finances and for the planning
- Letting your leader know your availability to help at Messy Vintage
- Attending team planning/training sessions, sharing ideas and helping with resources and preparations.
- Helping set up beforehand if possible
- Cooperating with requests from care home staff (if in that venue)

- Welcoming and chatting to guests, their families and members of staff
- Helping guests with the activity and enabling conversation around the theme as appropriate
- Joining in the celebration, leading it if required, and encouraging people to participate appropriately
- Serving the meal/tea if required and joining in with the guests
- Helping to clear up afterwards
- Providing feedback to the leader on how the session went and on any thoughts, stories, significant conversations (that can be shared without breaching confidentiality), changes or suggestions.

If you would like to know more or to join in, please contact your Messy Vintage team leader:

Name: ....

Tel: ....

Email: ....

Thank you!

This appendix is available to download at **messychurch.org.uk/messy-vintage**.

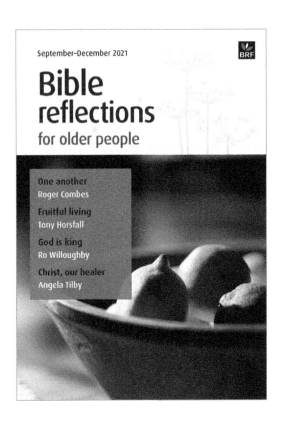

September–December 2021

Bible reflections
for older people

One another
Roger Combes

Fruitful living
Tony Horsfall

God is king
Ro Willoughby

Christ, our healer
Angela Tilby

Written for older people, these reflections are designed to bring hope, assurance and sustenance, reminding the reader of the presence and love of God. In each issue are 40 Bible reflections and prayer suggestions to use and revisit as often as is needed. In the central section, Debbie Thrower of BRF's Anna Chaplaincy ministry offers interviews and ideas to encourage and inspire. *Bible Reflections for Older People* is published every four months – in January, May and September.

Bible Reflections for Older People
Edited by Eley McAinsh
£5.25 per issue

brfonline.org.uk

Seriously Messy

Making space for families to talk
together about death and life

**Joanna Collicutt, Lucy Moore,
Martyn Payne and Victoria Slater**

When families experience bereavement and loss, it can be hard for the
wider church community to know how best to support them. In this
book, four experienced authors and practitioners offer intergenerational
approaches for engaging with questions of death and life in a safe and
supportive setting. The material guides church communities who are
dealing with the death of loved ones and other situations of loss in talking
together as a church family, in applying the Christian message of the
resurrection in challenging situations, and in listening to each other and
developing their own insights.

Seriously Messy
Making space for families to talk together about death and life
Joanna Collicutt, Lucy Moore, Martyn Payne and Victoria Slater
978 0 85746 823 9 £8.99

brfonline.org.uk

Bible readings for
special times

Ill Health
Wendy Bray

Whether we are going through a period of being house-bound through ill
health or facing a short or longer stay in hospital, we can find help and
consolation in the Bible. This book offers 24 undated reflections drawing
on a range of relevant Bible passages, and offering ways of connecting
more closely with God and drawing strength, peace and security from the
knowledge of his presence with us.

Ill Health
Bible readings for special times
Wendy Bray
978 0 85746 231 2 £3.99

brfonline.org.uk

Anxious Times

Carmel Thomason

Foreword by Archbishop John Sentamu

A book of 24 undated reflections drawing on a range of relevant Bible passages to offer genuine hope and encouragement in anxious times. Encompassing the very human emotions of fear and anxiety, the reflections encourage us to draw comfort and strength from God's word even in those times when he seems silent to us. This book acknowledges that trust and hope in God's goodness doesn't always come easily, but when embraced we gain the strength to face our fear with courage and confidence.

Anxious Times
Bible readings for special times
Carmel Thomason
978 0 85746 660 0 £4.99

brfonline.org.uk

Bereavement

Jean Watson

This book of 24 undated reflections draws comfort and inspiration from the Bible and from experience for those who are going through a time of bereavement, as well as providing insight for those wanting to support others who are bereaved. Jean Watson suggests how it might feel to get through the dark days and to move, however slowly, from 'getting by' with help, to 'getting a life' in which living with loss goes alongside the gains in terms of new insights on faith and life and a greater ability to empathise with others.

Bereavement
Bible readings for special times
Jean Watson
978 0 85746 326 5 £3.99

brfonline.org.uk

In this unique book, Wanda Nash, a well-established writer on spirituality in her late 70s, reflects on growing old with faith and a positive spirit. This compelling invitation to grow old boldly – full of her own experiences and insights – includes Wanda's reflection on her encounter later in life with terminal cancer, and her thoughts on coping with the daily challenges of living a Christian life in her illness and in ageing. Demonstrating a profound sense of the value and purposefulness of 'old age', the author's indomitable spirit is matched only by her fresh vision of the love of God in Jesus Christ.

Come, Let Us Age!
An invitation to grow old boldly
Wanda Nash
978 0 85746 558 0 £6.99

brfonline.org.uk

Enabling all ages to grow in faith

Anna Chaplaincy

Living Faith

Messy Church

Parenting for Faith

100 years of BRF

2022 is BRF's 100th anniversary! Look out for details of our special new centenary resources, a beautiful centenary rose and an online thanksgiving service that we hope you'll attend. This centenary year we're focusing on sharing the story of BRF, the story of the Bible – and we hope you'll share your stories of faith with us too.

Find out more at **brf.org.uk/centenary**.

To find out more about our work, visit

brf.org.uk